I
Just
Wanted
to
Save
My
Family

STÉPHAN PÉLISSIER

WITH CÉCILE-AGNÈS CHAMPART

translated from the French by Adriana Hunter

OTHER PRESS / NEW YORK

I
Just
Wanted
to
Save
My
Family

A Memoir

Originally published in 2019 as *Je voulais juste sauver ma famille*
by Éditions Michel Lafon, Neuilly-sur-Seine Cedex, France.
Copyright © Éditions Michel Lafon, 2019
English translation copyright © Other Press, 2021

Poetry excerpt on page 153 from "Condemned Women: Delphine and
Hippolyta" in *The Flowers of Evil* by Charles Baudelaire, translated by
James McGowan. Copyright © James McGowan 1993. Oxford University Press,
Oxford, England. Epigraph on page 183 from *The Trial* by Franz Kafka,
translated by Mike Mitchell. Copyright © Mike Mitchell 2009.
Oxford University Press, Oxford, England.

Production editor: Yvonne E. Cárdenas
Text designer: Jennifer Daddio/Bookmark Design & Media Inc.
This book was set in Horley Old Style and Helvetica Neue
by Alpha Design & Composition of Pittsfield, NH

1 3 5 7 9 10 8 6 4 2

Library of Congress Cataloging-in-Publication Data
Names: Pélissier, Stéphan, author. | Champart, Cécile-Agnès, author. |
Hunter, Adriana, translator.
Title: I just wanted to save my family : a memoir / Stéphan Pélissier ;
with Cécile-Agnès Champart ; translated from the French by Adriana Hunter.
Other titles: Je voulais juste sauver ma famille. English.
Description: New York : Other Press, [2021] | "Originally published in 2019
as Je voulais juste sauver ma famille by Éditions Michel Lafon,
Neuilly-sur-Seine Cedex."
Identifiers: LCCN 2020021949 (print) | LCCN 2020021950 (ebook) |
ISBN 9781635420180 (paperback) | ISBN 9781635420197 (ebook)
Subjects: LCSH: Pélissier, Stéphan—Family. | Pélissier, Stéphan—Trials, litigation,
etc. | Refugees—Syria—Biography. | Human smuggling—Greece. |
False imprisonment—Greece. | Lawyers—France—Biography. |
Syria—History—Civil War, 2011—Refugees. | France—Emigration
and immigration—Government policy.
Classification: LCC HV640.5.S97 P45 2021 (print) | LCC HV640.5.S97 (ebook) |
DDC 956.9104/231 [B]—dc23
LC record available at https://lccn.loc.gov/2020021949
LC ebook record available at https://lccn.loc.gov/2020021950

To my wife,

ZENA

To my daughters,

JULIA AND MILA

Contents

I
Just
Wanted
to
Save
My
Family

1. Damascus (Syria) – Beirut (Lebanon),
by coach, 115 km

2. Beirut – Tripoli (Lebanon),
by coach, 81 km
Tripoli (Lebanon) – Mersin (Turkey),
by boat, 370 km

3. Mersin – Bodrum (Turkey) – Izmir (Turkey),
by coach, 1070 km

4. İzmir – Sığacık Mahallesi (Turkey),
on foot, approximately 40 km
Sığacık Mahallesi – Samos (Greece),
by inflatable boat + coast guard boat,
approximately 100 km

5. Samos – Athens (Greece),
by water bus, 430 km

6. Athens – Patras (Greece),
by car with Stéphan, 210 km

7. Patras – Thessaloniki (Greece) –
Macedonia – Belgrade (Serbia),
by coach, 1130 km

8. Belgrade – Budapest (Hungary),
on foot and by coach, 420 km

9. Budapest – Vienna (Austria),
in people smugglers' cars and
by taxi, 240 km

10. Vienna – Munich (Germany),
by train, 430 km
Munich – Berlin (Germany),
by coach, 600 km

11. Berlin – Luxembourg – Paris (France),
by train, 1100 km

First of All

My name is Stéphan Pélissier. I'm forty-seven years old. I live in Albi, a small town in southwest France, with my wife, Zena, and our two young daughters. I go to work, pay off my mortgage, and on Sundays we often go to my parents' house for roast chicken.

As you can see, my life is unremarkable, ordinary, and that's the way I like it.

I'm just like any other Frenchman.

But I'm also a criminal who was condemned to seven years' imprisonment by the Greek justice system in November 2017.

My only crime was wanting to save my family: refusing to abandon my in-laws and their children to certain death as they tried to flee their native country, Syria, which had been torn apart by a conflict that has killed hundreds of thousands of people and sent millions more into exile.

An ordinary Frenchman surrounded by a loving family.

A Syrian woman, a brilliant lawyer who wanted to complete her studies in France, a country she'd always loved.

And her parents, caught in the vise of civil war and then the horrors of an escape with a very uncertain outcome, buffeted between grasping human-smugglers and inhuman laws.

These are the people you will meet in this book.

This is my story, it is our story. And when you have finished reading it, I hope you will feel it is yours too.

1.

Wedding(s)

What are you doing, Stéphan? We're going to be late!"

This must be the tenth time I've tied my tie today, but I can't get it right. I do it often enough, except that today I'm not just going to a meeting. I'm getting married.

Two little knocks at the door, and my mother comes in. She finds me facing the mirror in my bedroom in the family home, dressed impeccably from head to foot but with my tie still askew. I'm starting to lose patience. My mother instantly understands the problem.

"Give it to me, darling, your father will fix it."

He taught me in the first place, he's mastered this art. She soon comes back with a perfectly knotted tie, and I'm immediately calmer. I catch my mother looking at me in the mirror, full of pride and emotion. This gives me a chance to look at her too, my mother, my mom, the woman who gave me the love that allows me in turn to love. She's dressed beautifully today, radiant with happiness and more than a little relief: She was starting to worry because I still wasn't married at thirty-nine.

"You'll be down soon, won't you?"

I just need to arrange my pocket square and I'll be ready. I'm marrying the most beautiful woman in the world, so the least I can do is perfect my appearance.

My fiancée isn't far away: While I've battled with my tie, Zena has been dressing in my parents' bedroom, helped by her Serbian friend, Yelena. My bride-to-be will wear a dress we bought together in Nancy. Not very traditional! Just like our story so far, in fact . . .

I race down the stairs four at a time. A minute later Zena comes down too. I gaze at her, so beautiful in her long bustier dress that accentuates her spectacular figure. She's wearing simple pearl earrings and a necklace of fine lace. To my way of thinking, it's obvious: A Hollywood star is coming toward me, smiling. The gentle *toot* of a car horn brings me back to the moment. The rental car has come to take us to the *Mairie*—the town hall.

All our guests are waiting outside. It's a short list: my close family and my closest friends, about thirty of us in all. Because my future wife's family can't join us for the big day, I'm very glad Yelena is here with her.

My father takes my fiancée's arm, and my mother takes mine, and that's how we make our entrance at Castelginest's *Mairie*. My father has put on his red, white, and blue sash. We are especially lucky: As Castelginest's town councillor, he will conduct our marriage ceremony. This makes me very happy, and I hope it's a source of pride for a man I've always been afraid of disappointing.

"Come in, my friends!" he says in a powerful voice, and our little gathering settles into the *Mairie*'s only room. Zena and I stay standing, side by side, facing my father, who has donned his glasses to read to us from the civil code. But before he starts, he puts the text down for a moment and looks at us.

"My children, I'm the happiest of men this morning: I have the pleasure of officiating the marriage of my son, Stéphan, to the woman he loves. Not only am I witnessing my son's happiness, I also have the pleasure of welcoming Zena into our family. I know what's happening in Syria, and I'm painfully aware of what your parents are going through. Welcome, Zena, you will be like a daughter to me now."

The exchange of vows will be imprinted on my memory for the rest of my days. Although we're speaking to my father, Zena and I turn to face each other, and our *Yeses* echo in the small hall. Zena's is serious and gentle, mine resonant and vibrant. Caught up in the momentousness of our promises, neither of us smiles.

After posing for a few photographs in the *Mairie*'s garden, we all head for the restaurant near Toulouse that we've rented out for the occasion. The order of the day is a very simple reception with a few speeches, music—some of it Greek, some of it Middle Eastern—and champagne. I stand up to speak just before dessert.

"Dear friends and family, thank you for being here today! My darling, I'm so happy to be your husband, even though I still don't know how I got you to fall in love with me. It's a miracle, but God is great, every religion says so!"

My friends laugh out loud and Zena smiles.

"Thank you for coming to be with us today," I continue, "some of you from a long way away. I'd like to remember those who are no longer with us, who we wish were here. And also people dear to me who couldn't join us: my wife's family. A special thank you to my close family: my sister, Sandra; my niece, Charlotte; and you, my parents. Lastly, of course I want to talk about the woman who became my wife today. Zena, I'd like to pay tribute to you for your sensitivity, your erudition, your cooking, and your strong personality, and of course I must mention your physical beauty and your inner beauty. I would like to honor your culture by reading an extract from the holy Koran, sura 113:

> *"Daybreak—Al Falaq*
> *"I take refuge with the Lord of Daybreak, from*
> *the evil of what He created, and from the evil of the*

darkness as it gathers, and from the evil of those who
practice sorcery, and from the evil of the envious when
he envies."

Now it's Zena's turn to stand, and her whole body seems to be quivering with emotion.

"I'd like to thank my parents-in-law, Claude and Marianne, and my sister-in-law, Sandra. They've welcomed me and taken me in as one of the family. They respect who I am and my origins. My thoughts are also with those who are far away but are always in my heart: my parents, whom I love so much. They have accepted my choices and trusted me. They love Stéphan and have welcomed him as he is. Lastly, I'd like to thank you, Stéphan, the man who is now my husband. I love how sensitive you are, and I love your strong character too—as you all know, sparks can fly with us two! I promise I will be faithful, loving, and true to you."

My wife sits down amid the applause, looks at me, and kisses me. "To the happy couple!" reverberates around the room, not for the first time, as the restaurant manager brings in the wedding cake, which was delivered by the local patisserie this morning. In pride of place at the top of this sculpted confection stand a tiny bride and groom in pulled sugar.

My head's spinning a little, if I'm honest. Zena's eyes, the champagne, my friends' smiles, children laughing as they run between the tables...And it all happened so quickly! To think that fifteen months ago I hadn't even met Zena...

At nearly thirty-eight, I'd been invited to most of my friends' weddings and had watched them start families one after another. Meanwhile, although I couldn't say why, it hadn't happened for me. I'd had a few serious relationships in between long periods on my own. Either way, I'd never felt ready to commit forever, and the breakups had been painless enough to convince me I'd made the right decision. I hadn't given up, though. I was still hoping the right person was out there for me somewhere. So I regularly signed up for dating sites for a few weeks, met someone I liked, and then returned to the site once I was single again.

In late April 2011 I logged onto another dating site, full of my usual optimism. I perused the site and, almost intuitively, felt I should check "all of France" rather than restricting myself to the Toulouse region, as I had always done. A photo of a beautiful stranger appeared, a black-and-white portrait completely dominated by her incredible eyes. I got lost in them for a moment before noticing that the young woman, whose username was Venus, lived in Nancy. More than eight hundred kilometers away. Not very sensible, but who cared? So I sent a message to introduce myself. Venus's answer didn't keep me waiting long, but it had the effect of a cold shower:

> Venus: I've just had a look at your profile before answering and I really don't like the way you operate. I'm looking for a serious relationship, I refuse to be with someone who's not only already in a relationship but, worse than that, doesn't say so clearly.
>
> Me: I don't understand! I'm single, I promise!
>
> Venus: Of course you are . . . but you're hoping to meet someone a long way away from where you live and you use a profile photo where it's obvious there's a young woman standing next to you.

What an idiot! I looked closely at my profile photo and she was right: Next to me, as I stood there grinning, was a woman's shoulder and a tumble of long black hair. It was just my sister, Sandra. The picture had been taken at a baptism, and it was the only decent one I had of myself. I'd cropped the image as best I could, but that wasn't enough. Okay, so I now had to convince Venus that I was genuine.

> Me: That's my sister next to me in the photo, it was taken at a family party. I'm looking for a serious relationship too, and if you give me the chance, if you'll agree to meet me, I'm sure you'll believe me.
>
> Venus: I don't know. I need to think about it.
>
> Me: Okay. Take your time! Speak soon, I hope.

For the next three days of feverish waiting, she was all I could think about. Then, finally, Venus contacted me again, suggesting I call her. I was over the moon and did everything I could to prepare for that phone call. When she picked up, I forgot everything I'd planned and lost myself in the sound of her voice. We talked for nearly two hours, but the time just flew by. A few phone calls later, Venus agreed to a Skype call. When the connection was made, I was struck by the contrast between our two faces on the screen. I had a huge, very nervous smile—even I thought that I was overdoing it a little. Meanwhile, she eyed me imperiously (although she later admitted she was just as nervous as I was). I can't remember what I said during that conversation, just that I was hopeless and awkward but sincere and open. When she ended the call after about twenty minutes, I was the happiest of men: I finally knew her real name. "My name's Mouzayan, but everyone calls me Zena."

In the space of a few weeks we got to know each other over the phone and on Skype. Zena told me she was Syrian—I didn't know anyone from her country—and had been studying at Nancy University since 2007. She already had two master's degrees in law and was now working on a thesis on penal law. She was, in fact, already a lawyer in Syria. Her parents had brought her up with a taste for French culture, and like her brothers and sisters she'd been learning to speak French since she was four. After a first very brief marriage (which ended in divorce a few months later), Zena wanted to experience life in France and pursue her studies in more detail, having already excelled as the valedictorian of the law school at the University of Damascus. She had qualified as a graduate teaching assistant in Damascus, taken a language exam to confirm that she would be able to study in France, and secured a grant from the Syrian government to go to Nancy University.

After two or three more Skype conversations, we wanted to meet for real. We decided to rendezvous in Lyon, a city we both wanted to visit and that was more or less equidistant from each of us. I arrived a few hours before she did and planned to be waiting at the end of the platform when she alighted from her train. I don't know how I managed this, but I got to the platform late—my trademark, according to Zena. In the end we met in the station's corridors. My first thought was, "Not a chance, Stéphan, it'll never work. She's too beautiful for you. Way too beautiful for you." Her profile photo, and even what I'd seen of her on Skype, hadn't prepared me for the gorgeous woman walking toward me. By the end of our weekend in Lyon, I was hopelessly in love, and when I took Zena back to the station, I didn't want to waste any time.

"If you're ok with it, I'll come to Nancy next weekend."

She was stunned, and I noticed her hesitate for a moment.

"I . . . yes, ok. Come."

After that, it all happened very quickly.

We decided that, after we were married, we would live together, so before the wedding Zena came down to join me in Toulouse, and then we moved to Albi, where I worked most of the time, which meant I had more time to be with Zena. The fact that she was a PhD student meant she didn't need to live in Nancy; she could work just as well in the southwest, and could get on a plane when she needed to see her adviser.

We started talking about getting married six months after we met. Zena was able to meet my parents at a very early stage, and we both felt that it was important that she officially introduce me to her parents before the wedding in Castelginest. My dearest wish was to travel to Damascus, but, with the Syrian civil war raging, I couldn't get a visa. Meanwhile, Zena's parents soon realized that they couldn't secure the necessary permission to come to the ceremony in France. Zena then came up with the idea of arranging not only a meeting but a real wedding celebration in the Lebanese capital, Beirut, which is only about a hundred kilometers from Damascus.

So here we are, at the start of July 2012 in a taxi taking us from the airport to our hotel, in the Hamra neighborhood of Beirut. Manal, Zena's sister, came to meet us, having arrived the day before with her husband, Khaled, and their children. Zena chats happily with her sister. She hasn't stopped smiling since we got on the plane: She can't wait to see her family and watch them meet me. I know her parents have a sufficiently modern outlook to have supported their daughters just as much as their sons in their studies and career choices, but I'm anxious that cultural differences could mean they will have reservations about me. Zena told her father about me very soon after we met. Once he knew she was serious about the relationship, he voiced his qualms: Zena should finish her degree in Europe and go home to exercise her profession as a lawyer and university lecturer rather than settling in France—and what work would she get there, anyway? He could understand that she had feelings for me, but it was a big leap to be considering marrying someone so different from her when she'd already had one failed marriage.

In other words, I'm not exactly heading into conquered territory.

It's Thursday evening and Zena's parents will be arriving on Saturday morning. Manal and Khaled have decided to spend the day with us on Friday to show us around the Beirut region. In glorious sunshine, we drive out of the capital and visit the coastal city of Jounieh. Zena and Manal have a thousand things to talk about, of course, and while they chat Khaled and I discover that we have a lot in common—it turns out we both work in law. Our conversation is animated.

"I try to stay optimistic, Stéphan, but I'm worried for my wife and kids. I'm known to be against the regime, and in my work, for the last eighteen months I've defended only objectors. That can't help winding some people up."

"Have you had threats?"

"More than once. Manal and I are holding out for now. If things get any worse, she wants to move to France."

"Well, if you reach that decision, you can count on us to help."

"Thank you, my friend. We haven't come to that yet, thank God. But I won't forget your offer."

After lunch we take a cable car, which affords breathtaking views over Jounieh bay and brings us to the town of Harissa, with its famous shrine, Our Lady of Lebanon. My Muslim in-laws are keen to show me this important site of Christian pilgrimage, demonstrating the genuine respect for other monotheistic religions that every true Muslim has.

I wake early the following morning, very conscious of how important the day ahead is. Zena and I are expecting her parents to arrive during the morning for the official introduction. I've had just one telephone conversation with her father a few weeks ago—I wanted to call him as a mark of respect.

They're late, but we're prepared for that: The road from Damascus to Beirut is punctuated with checkpoints that make progress very difficult and journey times impossible to predict. The telephone rings: It's reception letting us know that my fiancée's parents have finally arrived. We go down to meet them in the hotel lobby.

Zena does the introductions, starting with her father.

"Dad, this is Stéphan Pélissier, the man I've chosen to marry."

"Welcome to our family, Stéphan. Zena's told us so much about you, we're very happy to finally meet you."

Saif Eddine Al Khatib comes up to me, shakes my hand, and draws me toward him for a hug. His firm grip immediately communicates all the energy and determination that this man has already demonstrated so many times in his life.

"Mom, this is Stéphan, my future husband."

Wafaa Al Khatib looks at me but says nothing. Zena has warned me that she's extremely discreet and reserved. I pause for a moment, hesitant and embarrassed: Would it be appropriate and respectful for me to shake her hand or to kiss her? I hadn't thought to ask Zena about this! Rooted to the spot by this conundrum and paralyzed at the thought of committing a blunder, I stay where I am with my arms hanging limply, and it's Wafaa herself who comes to my rescue by stepping forward and taking my hand in hers while her face lights up with the kindest of smiles. I tell her quietly that I'm happy to meet her, and her soft warm hands communicate her kindliness and love as a mother more eloquently than any words could.

With Zena's parents are her other sisters, Mayada and Mirvat, and her younger brother, Anas. They exuberantly rush over to me as soon as the introductions to her parents are finished. We chat for a while, and they are as relaxed with me as they are speaking French.

Soon, we all head up to our suite, where Zena and I busy ourselves serving refreshments. I notice Wafaa is now carrying a huge dish of vine leaves stuffed with rice. I'm overwhelmed with emotion because this dish encapsulates my childhood, it's what my Greek maternal grandmother, Voula Paraskevi, used to make for me all the time! Granny called them dolmas—here they say *yalanji*, but when I taste them, I rediscover the exact same pleasures of this simple yet delicious dish: the moist rice, the soft crunch of the leaves, the combination of hot spices and cool mint…In a flash I'm nine years old again, sitting at Granny's little kitchen table, and she's watching me eat my favorite food with my fingers while she tells me a story from my mother's childhood. This dish is my family, and here it is being served by the family of the woman I'm going to marry. This is wonderful, it's the universe giving us its blessing.

The whole family has arranged to meet at a restaurant at seven o'clock. We're on the Corniche Beirut, a wide seafront esplanade on the promontory with incredible views over the Mediterranean. Nearby, the old lighthouse—a tall, tapering building with black and white stripes—seems to watch over us. Zena has changed into a cream-colored silk dress with a light matching wrap, and her hair is held in a headband embellished with feathers that form a flower shape. She's radiant. This first evening will be the most private: only Zena's parents, her sisters, brother, and other members of her close family are invited. We walk through the front of the restaurant and at the back we find a pretty terrace with sea views. We all take our seats around the spread of salads, grilled meats, and other mezze, looking forward to a family feast. It's a very enjoyable meal, with a succession of different groups at each table as we regularly swap places to keep the conversation varied. After dinner we go back inside, where a room has been reserved for us to dance the night away.

For Zena and me, this evening isn't just a party: It really is a ceremony, a sacred moment in our relationship. We now tell our friends and family—including our daughters—that we were married in July 2012, first in Beirut and then in Castelginest a few days later. After this intimate party at the restaurant, we continue celebrating our union with friends and family for the next two days, but it's this first evening that's really imprinted on my heart.

These are the best days of our lives so far and we should be completely happy...

But our parents haven't even met, and that's something we must accept.

But Zena can't show me her country, and that's something we must accept.

But her parents can't see what her life is like in France, and that's something we must accept.

Because our love is powerless in the face of a violent civil war that erupted just when our relationship first started.

In April 2011, when we were exchanging our first emails, Syria saw an unprecedented wave of protests. The regime's reaction was swift and brutal: Demonstrators were shot at with live bullets and tortured, and thousands of people were taken in for questioning.

In July 2012, while we were celebrating our marriage, the conflict grew fiercer and more entrenched, with the repression of protesters increasingly savage. And the Islamic State took advantage of this chaos to advance on Syria.

How could we hope this conflict wouldn't affect us?

How could we think this war would have no consequences for all of us, from Damascus all the way to France?

2.

Four thousand kilometers

After our wedding, Zena and I settle into the same happy routine enjoyed by millions of couples in France. We love each other and we have plans: to have children and build a house. But there's a permanent shadow hovering over our happiness. Knowing that Zena's family is so far away and so beyond our reach . . . it's tough for me but much worse for my wife. French television channels present us with terrible images of the conflict tearing her country apart. Week after week there are more reports about demonstrations being quashed with appalling bloodshed, and about armed conflict between the rebel army and government forces. Sitting and watching our screen at home, all we feel is sheer rage at our powerlessness and terror that our loved ones are in danger.

When we next see Zena's family, in Beirut in March 2013, Zena is four months pregnant. We're both very happy and have set our hearts on telling them the news in person. But oh, the contrast between our quiet lives and what Wafaa and Saif are going through: Not long after our wedding, they had to move because their lovely apartment on the outskirts of Damascus ended up in a war zone. My heart constricts as Saif describes the cramped accommodations they managed to find at very short notice, and their landlord who takes delight in ramping up the rent—war creates a lot of casualties, and a handful of fortunes. Zena and I ask them—the first of many times—to leave their country to join us in France. She and I talked about it all through our flight, and she naively thought that our unborn child would clinch the argument, persuading them to flee. But, convinced that they are safe in the center of Damascus, Saif refuses to give in to terror. It will be more than a year before he makes up his mind to ask France for help, to no avail.

Zena is devastated. Fear eats away at her. Week after week, month after month, the situation in Syria worsens. My wife is losing sleep over it, traumatized by images on TV and social networks. I, meanwhile, am outraged. I wish Saif and all of his family could join us as soon as possible, but I understand his indignation: No human being should have to flee his or her own home to escape bombing. And when it does come to that, they shouldn't have to plead with a peaceful country to save their lives. Either way, there's nothing I can do. Nothing. And it's driving me crazy. I can't reassure my wife, she has so many reasons to worry. I can't take her family out of harm's way, it's not in my power. I can only ball my fists with rage as the TV shows me bombings, ravaged landscapes, civilian victims, exiles... and the unshakeable, triumphant Bashar al-Assad.

3.

Living and growing up in Bashar al-Assad's Syria

ANAS'S STORY

I think I realized very early on that nothing in life happens as planned. I already thought about this a lot when I lived in Syria. Obviously, not many young people who live with their parents have hectic lives full of shocking surprises, but when you go to school in Damascus things are very different.

The civil war started when I was just thirteen, and I'd already had friends disappear overnight or come to school in tears because they'd lost a loved one—either killed in a confrontation or taken in one of the regime's arbitrary roundups. But my parents, my sisters, and I were convinced that we could and should stay in Damascus.

Looking back, I don't know how we held out for so long.

My parents were forced to move for the first time in 1997: The government had labeled their neighborhood an "area of historical interest" and had expropriated their house. They ended up, on very short notice, in Husseiniya, in the outlying southern suburbs of Damascus. Luckily, four years later my father managed to get a house not so far from central Damascus. But in 2012 they had to abandon that home, which was now in a war zone, and move to a tiny apartment closer to the city center. It was tough both psychologically—we'd lost a lot of our creature comforts—and financially—our landlord raised the rent every month because he knew we didn't have a choice. Even so, we clung to the city where we had all been born, and the country for which my father had fought in his day. Stéphan and Zena kept saying we should leave Syria and join them in France, but my parents turned a deaf ear.

I'm not sure about my mother and sisters, but I stopped believing in the future when my father was abducted in 2014. Those four months when he was held prisoner have marked me for life. I couldn't understand how my mother stayed calm and always seemed optimistic. I could see she was sustained by her faith, and I was ashamed that I wasn't as pious as she was, ashamed that I was so terrified, thinking we'd never see my father again. Of course she was frightened too, especially at first, in the few days when we had no idea what had happened to him. Then came the ransom demand, and it may seem crazy, but we were relieved: So he hadn't been taken by the regime, which would have meant certain death. It was just a financially motivated kidnapping like so many others in Damascus at the time: Big wheels in their fifties and sixties were specifically targeted, and my father was just the sort of established figure with the means to pay an enticing ransom. Despite all my mother's efforts, it took a very long time to get him out. He was held for four months. When I finally saw him again, he had changed so much it felt like hugging my grandfather. After he came back, I couldn't bear it if anyone in the family was even five minutes late coming home. It gave me panic attacks.

We did a lot of talking as a family after that, and in the summer of 2014, finally persuaded, he agreed to ask for asylum for the whole family in France. The French embassy in Damascus had already closed, so he filed his request in Beirut.

When I went back to school in September 2014, my own life got a lot more complicated too. There were two gangs. Students whose parents were connected to the regime—and who therefore had the power—put the others, including me, through hell. I was regularly given death threats, insulted, pushed around, and beaten. I often went home bleeding, my face swollen and bruised, and my eyes half closed. I managed to hold back my tears only to avoid making my mother cry too. And anyway, my father hadn't cried.

At the end of 2014 the French consul in Beirut summoned my father to his office for a meeting about the request for asylum. The conversation went very well, my father made much of the fact that we'd all been learning French since we were very young and that two of my sisters were already in France. We were so happy: We would be granted asylum, for sure! But in March 2015, for reasons we simply couldn't understand, my parents received a terse email informing them that their application had been rejected.

How absurd: A month earlier, my sister Manal, her husband, and their children had received confirmation that France would grant them political asylum. But they'd been living on French soil for nearly two years, and they'd left Syria to live in Jordan even before that, shortly after Zena and Stéphan were married. It was in Jordan that my sister applied for and was given a precious D visa, which allowed her to go to France and ask for asylum. Manal worked as a translator for various NGOs in Amman, and she was able to use her contacts to secure a swift hearing and a positive outcome.

The situation in Damascus was growing steadily worse for us and everyone around us. My parents were increasingly concerned for their safety, for mine and for my future. I'd had excellent grades so far and wanted to focus on the sciences for my last two years at school but—here too—only the children of people connected to the regime had access to this option, the most prestigious in my country. I had no choice: I had to major in literature, which I found very boring, and the worst part was I knew it was robbing me of my dream of becoming an engineer.

One day at the start of summer 2015, just before dinner my father announced that he'd decided we must leave Syria and join our family in France. My mother and sisters were very worried: Without refugee status, we would have to rely on illegal and therefore dangerous migration networks. For me, though, it was quite simply the best possible news. I couldn't take any more of this life, and—at last—my father was giving me a glimpse of another future.

In the end, only Mirvat decided to stay. She wanted to finish her master's and could live with an uncle whose home was in a relatively safe neighborhood. Maybe she was also scared of the protracted journey itself, especially because she was exhausted at the time. My sister Mayada, whom everyone calls Mimo, would come on that journey with my parents and me.

The need for complete secrecy complicated preparations for our departure. If the authorities got wind of our plans, we risked being arrested before we even left the country. It would have been unthinkable to tell our landlord we were going abroad, we just said we were handing back the keys because the rent had become too expensive. I couldn't confide in friends at school, I couldn't even say goodbye to my two best friends, Fares and Mahmoud. As soon as I reached France, I contacted Fares to explain everything, but Mahmoud isn't on social media and I've never heard from him again.

A few days before we left, we sold everything. Everything. The journey would be very expensive, we had to pay for people smugglers, hotels, food...My father emptied all his bank accounts, and Manal and Zena sent us as much money as they could. My mother parted with bracelets, necklaces, and rings that she'd inherited from her family. I'm a real geek, so my most precious possessions were my game console and my computer: I sold them off within a few hours of putting an ad on social media. We changed all the money into euros and dollars, exchanging it in small sums to avoid attracting attention. We kept only our phones. I know some people are surprised when immigrants have the latest smartphone, but it's important to understand that during the grueling journey we were facing, phones would be our only means of communication. Because we would have no fixed abode until we reached France, it was imperative that we be able to contact not only our loved ones who'd stayed in Syria, but one another if we were separated. We would also needed our phones to use social media in order to find and contact the people smugglers who would get us over international borders. And we would use GPS apps on our phones to find our way around unfamiliar countries and cities. Not to mention the fact that the photos on my phone are now the only physical reminders of my life in Syria. I abandoned everything else when I left.

Just before leaving, we made the rounds among close family to say goodbye: my grandmother, aunts, uncles, and cousins. My aunt asked us to take her son Samer with us. He's the same age as me and we get along really well, but more importantly his mother knew that, like me, he had no future and no guarantee of safety in Syria. So Samer would be coming with us.

We took the bare minimum: a few clothes, our ID papers, and phones. We left everything else behind.

And we left.

In early August we buy flights from Beirut to Turkey from a travel agent. As Syrians, we don't need visas for this trip. On the morning of August 6, 2015, we climb into a bus to Lebanon and have no trouble crossing the border: My father has managed to obtain a pass for five people because our local mayor is a long-standing friend of his.

But once we get to the airport, huge disappointment: The flight we have tickets for just doesn't exist anymore! My father calls the travel agent and is told pertly that there may have been a mistake and we should come back to the airport at the same time tomorrow. Standing next to us in front of the departures board is another Syrian family in the same situation.

"What did they tell you?"

"To come back tomorrow, the flight's bound to go tomorrow."

"The liars, they're crooks! That's not how air travel works. Basically, we've been scammed."

"And if we come back tomorrow we're bound to be arrested."

"We can't stay here, it's too dangerous. We need to get to Turkey by sea."

We all set off to northern Lebanon to catch a bus heading for Tripoli. We spend the night there and catch a boat to Mersin, in Turkey, the next day. After sailing all night, we arrive at dawn. I haven't slept a wink, furious about the way we've been treated on the journey: the ground staff, the crew, they've all been so rude to us and to all the other Syrians on the boat. They've insulted us and pushed us around; they even shoved my mother to make her get onto the boat faster. And after they checked our passports, they threw them on the ground several paces away from us and sniggered when we ran to pick them up. So it's on this overnight crossing that I have my first taste of what we've become: subhuman, rootless, desperate creatures at the mercy of those we meet along the way. When I realize that we'll be subjected to this sort of treatment on a daily basis, my fury brings tears to my eyes. I'm all the angrier because I might have been expecting a chilly reception in

Europe, in countries with a very different culture from my own, but not in Lebanon! Yes, they say some Lebanese have hated the Syrians since the 1980s when Syrian forces first occupied Lebanon. But the Lebanese are our neighbors, our brothers! How can they treat us like this?

In Mersin, we go through simple formalities at the border to register that we are on Turkish soil, and then we're free to move about as we please. But we have no firm plans for the next step. We want to get into Greece, in the European Union, so now we have to tip onto the wrong side of the law. I've always known my parents to refuse even the most minor deceit, the mundane corruptions that are a part of everyday life in Syria, so it stresses me when I realize that we'll be breaking the law. Even to save my life, our lives. I so wish there was another way of doing this, without using illegal channels... We now spend hours every day on social media trawling for that rare gem: a reliable people smuggler who'll get us to Greece. Names, contact details, and prices are all there if you know where to look; you just need someone to sponsor you to join a secret Facebook group. In Syria, there's always a friend, neighbor, or cousin who's dealt with a people smuggler and can get you in. After that, it's like following a series of trails, switching from a group on Facebook to one on WhatsApp and so on. But there are lots of disappointments: false names; phone numbers that no one answers, perhaps because they've been arrested; and prices always much higher over the phone than advertised online. We naturally try to distinguish the good dealers from the bad by reading the personal accounts of refugees who succeeded in getting across.

We travel between the cities of Bodrum and İzmir a number of times, because these seem to be the two possible starting points. We meet several smugglers in both places, in a constant seesaw of hope and disappointment. This is my introduction to the world of crime and its brutality. Before we grasp the fact that there's no hope of leaving from Bodrum—it is a tourist hot spot and is too closely scrutinized by the authorities—we meet a local smuggler who says, Yes and it'll cost x and now we need to meet another guy, my associate who has the team who do the actual crossing. It turns out our contact doesn't really know the other man. When he takes us to the meeting, we find ourselves surrounded by a gang of beefy thugs. Armed with knives, they threaten to kill us if my father doesn't give them all the money we have. We hesitate for a split second and then run as fast as we can. Luckily not one of them sets off in pursuit—they may be criminals but they're lazy!

The days are trickling by and we're spending a lot of money on living expenses and scams. Our every conversation revolves around the longing to get out of Turkey as soon as possible, it's become an obsession for the five of us. We have to save every dollar and every euro so we have just two meals a day and we stay in crummy, dirty hotels in seedy neighborhoods where we constantly fear for our safety—especially when we often spend long hours after nightfall trying to find a hotel that will take us. Very often, even when Zena has booked something online, the manager throws us out, claiming that the place is full. Zena gets so mad when we tell her over the phone what's happened. Sometimes we try five or six hotels in one evening before we can settle in for the night. One time, we don't find anywhere till three in the morning. Another time, we give up in the end: We find a late-night restaurant and stay there until it closes, then wait on a bench till the first early-bird café opens.

In İzmir we finally meet what seems to be the right man, the people smuggler who will get us across the border to Greece. We come to an agreement with him: It will cost one thousand euros per person, and he tells us he'll take us right away, tonight, once it's completely dark. He warns us that he won't provide life jackets, we need to supply those ourselves. Not having them would be out of the question, obviously, and my parents buy one for each of us. This isn't difficult in İzmir, seemingly every shop sells them for about twenty euros each: The constant stream of refugees through town is a gold mine for them.

That evening about sixty of us gather at the agreed meeting place. The smuggler reassures us, saying we'll be divided into two groups in two very comfortable boats. And he explains that we won't be leaving from İzmir itself but from a more discreet spot on the opposite coast, in the southwest. This means we have to make our way through more than thirty kilometers of dense and very hilly forest with no light, to avoid being spotted. I try to tread carefully but the smuggling team keeps urging us to go quickly so I can't help stumbling. And I'm not the only one. I hear my mother stifle a cry nearby, and I help her up as best I can. Then I twist my ankle on something and fall heavily on my back. It leaves a deep wound, and the pain is unbearable. But we just have to keep going, whatever happens, so we keep going. When we finally get to the beach, it takes me a moment to realize what's going on . . . then I'm filled with horror.

There's only one boat. Just one. It's eight meters long. There are sixty of us: men, women, and children, including several babies, plus our bags.

My father turns to us, ashen.

"We may die tonight, but we'll all die together. And if we survive, we'll all survive together."

My mother, my sister, and Samer are crying. I have no tears, I'm just suddenly very cold and tell myself over and over: *There's no other solution, there's no going back. Syria means death. Here we have a chance.* Anyway, the smuggler's henchmen have positioned themselves between us and the forest, and they're threatening us with guns. So no one protests and no one refuses to board the boat. There's a resignation in the face of risks that no one would normally choose to take, and I see it so often during the course of our journey, on the faces of people fleeing for the same reasons we are. While we are waiting in line to climb into the boat, another passenger, also Syrian, approaches my father.

"I think I should warn you, my brother, the life jackets you have...they're fakes. They won't inflate, look."

He turns over the jacket my father is wearing and shows him that it's made of foam that will soak up water. It doesn't change much at this stage, we keep them on our backs regardless. I will learn later that many Syrians die at sea because of these fake life jackets that drag them underwater.

As we're boarding we realize that my father has lost his briefcase along the way. In it were our ID cards, passports, and other official documents we thought would be useful to have with us. Luckily, not our money: That is in a belt around his waist, under his clothes. I don't really react to the loss of our documents. In comparison to what lies ahead, what does it matter?

Once on the boat, we stand tightly packed, partly treading on our bags. For an absurd moment, I think we must look like pickles in a jar. I look at my mother's face, which is distorted with pain. Her arm has been hurting terribly since her fall and there's nothing I can do for her, which fills me with anger. The boat puts to sea before daybreak, and we all start praying we'll survive.

Most of the passengers are Muslim, and we join them in reciting verses from the Koran. There are a few Christians praying too. Our voices blend together, collectively turned toward heaven. The monotony of it soothes even the babies, not one of them cries. The Turkish coastguards in the distance have spotted us and set out in pursuit but can't catch us in time: We cross the boundary of territorial waters and, to our enormous relief, they turn back.

Some time later there is a sudden, dull crack under our feet: The bottom of the boat has broken open under our weight. We're starting to sink. There are screams of terror, voices shouting, "Throw out your bags!" I throw mine overboard, it only had a few clothes in it. Just before the boat sinks completely we hear an engine, and we're momentarily blinded by searchlights. Two boats are drawing alongside us, and some people instantly panic, thinking they're pirates who will take what little we have left. I'm almost the only English speaker on board and can reassure everyone.

"Stay calm!" I say. "It says 'coast guard' and they're flying the Greek flag. It's the Greek coast guard, we're saved!"

The Greeks are kind enough to keep families together as they divide us between their two boats, and once I'm safely on board with my parents, Mimo, and Samer, I take a moment to pray—silently this time. I know that God saved our lives tonight. Without Him, that precarious boat would never have carried us all the way to Greece. Without Him, no one would have reached us in time to save us.

The coastguards bring us ashore at dawn. They tell us we're on the island of Samos and we need to report to the local authorities so that our identities can be registered and we can be given travel passes to reach a refugee camp in Athens. We listen to their instructions, slightly dazed; we're exhausted, happy to be alive but in a terrible state of shock. My mother is cradling her arm. We examine it in daylight and find it's swollen and has gone completely blue—it's fractured. She grits her teeth to stop herself crying in front of us. As soon as we're alone we find the first café that's open where we can sit down and rest, charge our phones, and call Zena and Manal.

4.

We can't leave them to die!

Zena is pale. Her long slender hand clutching the phone to her ear shakes in spasms. This woman who is usually so talkative when she's on the phone to her parents hardly opens her mouth. Her eyes are closed and a tear rolls, very slowly, down her cheek. I put a hand on her arm, as much to offer what little comfort I can as to attract her attention. She opens her eyes and looks at me without seeing me.

"Tell me, Zena," I whisper, "what's going on?"

We've had no news of her parents since yesterday, for almost twelve hours. Twelve hours during which Zena hasn't slept or eaten, convinced that there could be only two explanations for this silence: They're dead or in prison. When the phone rang at seven o'clock this morning we were prepared for the worst.

I squeeze her arm gently and she seems to rally and see me at last. She says, "Wait" in Arabic—I've learned a few words as time's gone by—and puts down the phone.

"Zena, tell me what's happened to them."

"The people smuggler they found in Turkey . . . He piled I don't know how many of them into an inflatable boat so of course it didn't hold out and the boat went down!"

"Oh shit, no, I can't believe it . . . Are they all okay?"

Zena gives me a brief summary of their terrifying ordeal.

"And where are they now?"

"On Samos, in a café. But that's not what's upsetting me. I talked to my mother and she said my father can't take any more, he just wants to get here to us as soon as possible. So he's already been looking for people smugglers to get across to Ancona, in Italy, and it'll be on the same sort of boat they were just on."

"But that's way too dangerous. They need to go around through the Balkans. Did you talk to him?"

"Yes, I asked my mother to hand him the phone . . . but he just doesn't want to listen to any talk about the Balkans. Apparently, Hungary is terrible for migrants. He claims it would be too risky."

"But they already nearly drowned . . . This will be even worse, the crossing to Italy is three times as far. Doesn't he realize that?"

"He tells me it won't be the first time they've been in danger since they set out and he puts his trust in God to protect them. And anyway, this just has to end. He even said he can't stop thinking about giving up and going back to Syria…"

There's no way to get my father to see sense, to make him realize they're heading for certain death. He just talks about praying and trusting in God. I'm a believer. But I don't set God wild challenges. The way I see it, my father might as well jump from the roof of a thirty-story building, crying, "I trust in you, Allah, save me!"

When I tell Stéphan what they're planning to do, he gets more and more agitated. And then he says these words, words that will seal our fates:

"I'll go get them"

"What?"

"You heard me. I'll go get them. We'll make the crossing to Italy together but we'll take a proper boat, a ferry. They'll be able to do it if they're with me. I'm not staying here and leaving them to drown. All my papers are in order, I speak Greek, it'll work."

"Are you sure?"

Stéphan's suggestion has split me in two. The wife in me doesn't want him to go and take a risk that's so difficult to quantify, but the daughter and sister wishes he was already on his way so that my family don't risk their lives again.

"Absolutely sure. Go ahead and tell them, please. Don't let them move. I'm on my way."

I think quickly. If I tell my father that Stéphan's coming to get them, he'll refuse the help and be in even more of a hurry to find a people smuggler before anyone stops him. But my mother told me they should be going to Athens once they have their travel passes. My father's hesitating between finding a smuggler in Samos or waiting to do it in Athens. If he opts for Athens, that will hold them on Samos for two days: Anas has done some research, there are no boats to the capital before then. I explain my idea to Stéphan and call them back.

"If you really want to attempt a crossing, Dad, you at least have to find a good, reliable smuggler with a suitable boat. Go get registered in Athens, there's bound to be more choice and more smugglers there than on that little island!"

I leave Zena on the phone in the bedroom and go to the kitchen to make two coffees. I didn't really think before telling Zena that I'd set off to Athens to fetch her family. Now, I think it through for a moment. Is it really a good idea? I don't know, but it's the only one I have.

What I do know is that Zena's been wasting away for eighteen months as the situation has gradually worsened in Syria, even in Damascus, which until recently was relatively unscathed. She's stopped making progress on her dissertation. Only our little Julia can occasionally revive her smile. I have to face the facts: My wife is descending slowly but surely into depression.

What I do know is that Julia is still asleep in the bedroom right next to ours. She just turned two. For a few weeks now I've been wondering whether she knows what's going on. If I don't do something my daughter may never see her grandparents, aunt, and uncle again. I can't just stay on my sofa, liking and sharing photos and videos on social media, without doing anything. This is my family. If something happened to them, what would I tell my daughter when she grows up? "I didn't try to do anything, it was too dangerous for me." I would never be able to look her in the eyes.

What I do know is that the war over there is forcing thousands of Syrians to take any risk in the hope of finding somewhere where they can at least survive. How many fathers lead their families onto those cockleshell boats? How many tragedies are there behind the horrific images we've seen on social media since we've been tracking our family's progress—overturned boats, backpacks and empty life jackets drifting at sea...

While Zena negotiates with her father, I start researching the laws about helping migrants. It's impossible to glean any information for Greece, because all the results that come up are in Greek and I'd prefer not to put my trust in machine translation for something like this—I speak Greek, but I can't read it. I have no trouble finding the French regulations, and soon establish that you are not punished for helping undocumented immigrants with travel and accommodations if they are your relations. Greece is in Europe so it can't be all that different.

managed to persuade my father to go to Athens to find a people smuggler. That will take up just enough time for Stéphan to arrange to get there. I feel relieved and guilty in equal measure. I should be holding my husband back, I should be stopping him from leaving, but I can't, I want him to go. Persuading him against it would be like condemning my family to death. My mind's going around in circles, jumping from one thought to another, it feels like my head's about to explode. Luckily, Julia will wake soon, and Stéphan and I will be busy arranging his trip.

I must leave tomorrow at the latest. I don't want to run the risk of Saif Eddine finding a people smuggler before I'm on my way and Zena can tell them I'm coming. We have very little time, it's a long way to Ancona.

While we drink our coffee, I show Zena the first bits of research I've done into helping foreigners come into the country. She reacts instantly: "You'll need our family record book, Stéphan. Everything's recorded in there, including my parents' names. It's proof that they're your family." She puts it into my bag with my phone charger and various forms of ID.

Mayada told Zena they lost almost all their belongings because the boat sank, so my wife will spend part of the day buying new clothes for Anas, nonprescription pain-killers for their injuries, and anything else she can find that might be useful.

I, meanwhile, must contact my boss to explain why I need more time off. Because, yes, I used my official vacation time in July. I tell him it's a family matter and luckily my standing within the company means it's not a problem.

I go to the bank to take out as much cash as I can—I don't want to end up stuck over there because I've reached the spending limit on my bank card. Then I sit down at the computer to study the timetable for ferries from Ancona. Crossings to Greece are overnight and, because it's the tourist season, there are departures every evening. But it's impossible for one person to drive from Albi to Ancona without a break. And anyway, I wouldn't get there in time for the ferry tonight... so I'll stop off in Genoa. I reserve a B&B for the night.

Zena and I keep up our research on social media as well as government websites to try to evaluate the risks I'm taking. Despite our efforts, I can't get a clear idea of the situation. Either way, I won't go back on my decision.

5.

Reunited in Patras

Just before midday on August 20, 2015, I kiss my wife and daughter goodbye, sit behind the wheel of my car and drive to Genoa. It's not until four hundred kilometers later, when I stop to fill the tank with gas, that I notice I didn't think to take out Julia's car seat. I think that says a lot about the rushed, improvised nature of my decision to go. Before crossing the border to Italy, I realize I should contact my parents—I haven't yet told them anything about this undertaking. I decide to call my mother. I explain the situation and tell her what Zena's parents would risk if I don't go. I can tell she's frightened, but she doesn't make a single negative comment and does her best to disguise her concern.

"Will you let dad know, please?" I ask before hanging up.

In the past—particularly when I was a teenager and in my early days as an independent young man—she often acted as a mediator between my father and me. I'm not afraid of confrontation, or of his criticizing my plan or being hostile to it, but I want to focus on the action itself and keep up the energy that's taking me to Greece: I can't let anyone sow seeds of doubt or inspire an inkling of fear in my mind. True, with hindsight I feel maybe I should have discussed it with him, he could have given me advice. But for now I'll leave my mother to explain my plan.

I reach Genoa at nine in the evening. The driving has exhausted me and I'm glad I chose this simple, pretty place where I can have something to eat and, crucially, get to bed early. Until I reached the border, I called Zena every couple of hours, but once in Italy I stopped calling—too expensive. Before going to bed I call for news and I can sense all the anxiety and tiredness in her voice that she doesn't want me to hear...

I'm tired too when I wake in the morning. I spent more time visualizing a succession of catastrophic scenarios than sleeping. And my whole body is stiff from driving the day before. But I must set off again, the ferry leaves Ancona at five this afternoon and it won't wait for me. The journey is an ordeal: the roads are clogged with vacationers—to be expected at this time of year—and, with each passing kilometer, I start to doubt my chances of succeeding. I have to shake myself regularly to stop from falling asleep or descending into overwhelming pessimism. Zena and I talk on the phone for a few minutes every couple of hours and, despite our fears, we manage to support each other somehow, especially because I can always hear Julia babbling in the background, which does me good.

At last I drive onto the ferry in Ancona. It feels slightly surreal. I'm struggling to take in the fact that I'm here on this boat, the same one that I hope to catch on the way back in two days' time with my wife's family. There are crowds of people around me, mostly tourists, couples, families on vacation, a few Greeks heading home. A lot of happiness and laughter, children running around, overexcited by what must be their first ferry crossing. And here am I carting around my fears and loneliness. I do what I can to concentrate on how happy I'll be when I see Saif, Wafaa, and the others, and the contentment that will be restored once everyone is safely in France.

My cabin is tiny but all I need is a cool shower and a bed. Exhausted by driving and my sleepless night in Genoa, I fall asleep just after we set sail.

I wake before dawn the next morning and the ferry arrives in the port of Patras a few hours later. I'm fidgety with impatience, but I'll have to wait to be reunited with my Syrian family: It takes more than two hours to disembark all the vehicles in the already crushing heat. Then, as I leave the port, I realize that my phone contract won't let me use the GPS outside of France. Most of the road signs are written in Greek, and I have trouble finding my way. I can't read Greek but, thank goodness, I speak it very well because Granny Voula lived with my family for ten years. She raised me when my parents were away: My policeman father traveled a lot for his work and my assistant-nurse mother often worked nights and weekends. My grandmother never learned more than a few words of French and only ever spoke to us in Greek. After she died, my mother reestablished contact with her family in Crete and I kept up my Greek by speaking with my uncle and cousins, but I never would have guessed that I would use the language as I am today, asking passersby how to get to Athens!

It takes me nearly four hours to get to the hotel in the Pasalimani neighborhood of Athens where Zena tells me her family is staying. She's given me Anas's phone number, and I've been talking to him as I drive toward the city. When I reach the hotel, he's out on the sidewalk waiting for me—he particularly wanted to be there when I arrived. I take him in my arms and hug him for a long time, lost for words. He leads me inside to see the rest of the family. They almost can't believe I'm there, jumping to their feet and hugging me, all of us filled with inexpressible emotion. We laugh and cry at the same time and when I call Zena we all talk at once, fizzing with happiness. I can reassure her because I think they all look to be in pretty good shape. My only concern is for my mother-in-law, whose arm is very swollen and bruised. But Anas tells me that ever since they lost most of their clothes when the boat went down, she's the one who—every evening and without a word of complaint—takes pride in washing the things they need for the next day.

We have a very simple dinner in Athens: The two boys take responsibility for going out and buying some souvlaki, Greek sandwiches of pita bread and skewer-grilled meat served with sliced tomato, onion, tzatziki, and fries. Saif has reserved two rooms for the six of us: Mayada will sleep with her parents and I'll be with Samer and Anas. We all eat together in Zena's parents' room. During the meal Saif describes their journey from Damascus and Anas does his best to translate in a combination of French and English that only he and I understand. It's strange, but we have no desire to leave our rooms this evening; we're together, packed in close—nothing can happen to us, we're invincible! Once we've moved into our own room, Samer, Anas, and I have a real boys' evening of music and videos on our phones . . . and a lot of laughter.

We all meet very early for breakfast the next morning. Mayada and Wafaa look gorgeous, having spent time and attention on their hair and makeup, and wearing the clothes that Zena bought for them. They haven't covered their hair: For our ferry crossing later, the intention is to pass ourselves off as a group of Europeans. We load everything into the trunk of my Dacia and set off for Patras just before eight o'clock. I try to think of everything without looking worried, but I have no idea we're about to have the longest day of our lives.

6

Arrest

fell asleep very quickly last night, soothed by the happiness I'd heard in the muddle of voices coming from my husband, parents, brother, and sister. But I woke at two in the morning in a bed soaked with sweat. What if it doesn't work? What if they're stopped? What if... what if... I couldn't get back to sleep.

I have my first ordeal this morning. Stéphan made an arrangement with his mother when he called to tell her he was going to Greece: She and Claude are going to lend us a mattress for the double bed we bought in anticipation of my family moving in with us. My sister-in-law, Sandra, has texted me to let me know that she and her parents are coming over this morning to bring it to me, with the help of an uncle—it's Sunday so everyone is free. I'm dreading their visit because I know what Stéphan's father is like, and I figure he won't be at all happy that his son didn't consult him or even warn him before he set off.

My father-in-law has hardly set foot through the door before he starts talking to me as he never has before, extremely aggressively.

"Why didn't he call me? It's completely idiotic, and I'll tell him myself, he'll know what I think when he gets back! Do you have any idea of the risks he's taking?"

His voice gets louder with each sentence and he doesn't give me a chance to reply. My mother-in-law is embarrassed, staring at her shoes in silence. Meanwhile, exhausted and overwhelmed, I dissolve into tears.

Looking back, I can understand my father-in-law's reaction: As a former policeman he had no trouble imagining all the problems his son would encounter, and he was frightened for his safety, for his life...

Luckily, the telephone rings and it's Stéphan. My mother-in-law is still gentle and kind to me, and I show her where the mattress needs to go before finding somewhere private to talk to my husband.

On the way from Athens to Patras, we talk a lot about strategy and come up with what we think is a good plan. As we see it, the key moment will be buying the ferry tickets. Of course it will be, because it's an international journey so it must be like flying and our documents will be checked before we're given the tickets. Well, documents...I'm the only one who can provide any because my Syrian family lost all of theirs before they reached Greece. So we'll have to find a way to prove our credentials, and this task will be achieved by Mayada and me: We're going to play the part of the perfect couple! My pretty sister-in-law has fair skin and could easily pass for a Westerner, and I have shaved carefully and I'm wearing a jacket for the occasion. At the ticket office I hand over my nice, polite Frenchman's passport and—in Greek— ask for six adult tickets. With the supplement for my car this comes to just over a thousand euros. The saleswoman doesn't ask for any supporting documents, not even the names of my fellow passengers. I pay in cash and leave with Mayada, a smile on my lips.

I don't want to show my feelings while we're still near the ticket office, but, as far as I can see, we did it! These tickets mean we'll definitely make the crossing. I just need to call Zena and give her the good news. With hindsight, I'm staggered by my own naivety. My wife sounds strained on the phone, and explains that my parents are there—I guess that my father has made it clear to her how displeased he is. I can't bear knowing how low she's feeling because we're euphoric on our end. It's nearly midday and we now need to wait until the boat sails at three. We find a table at a café opposite the huge steel gate at the entrance to the port's boarding area. The six of us are so happy, snapping photos of one another while we wait for our ke-babs. When Anas pours me a glass of wine he accidentally spills the carafe over himself and ends up shirtless, which makes Mayada, Samer, and me laugh uproariously.

Alone at last! And I've managed to have a nice lunch with my little girl. Before they all left I took the time to explain why Stéphan went and to outline the plan he's concocted to bring everyone back to France safely. I'm not sure I convinced any of them but just trying made me feel better.

It's not yet three o'clock but more and more cars are waiting to board outside the huge metal gate that opens and closes for every car. We can't see the ferry from here, it's a few hundred meters beyond the gate. Not wanting to worry my traveling companions, I don't show my concern as I watch the succession of cars slipping through the gate one at a time...and start to realize that we greatly underestimated the checking system for departures. I can see that showing tickets isn't enough: Car trunks are inspected by a team of men in civilian dress working in relays along the line. This is invariable, every trunk is searched, but that doesn't trouble me much—we have nothing to hide in the trunk of my Dacia. What I'm much

more concerned about is the fact that these men checking cars are definitely not employed by the ferry company.
As I reach this conclusion, I notice that the car currently
waiting outside the gate is, in fact, being subjected to a
more in-depth search: It looks as if the driver is handing
over documents and passports. I see him rifling through
further documents in a bag and gesticulating wildly at the
man checking his paperwork. A cold shiver runs down my
spine. They're policemen, clearly. The police. How could
I think there wouldn't be police checks when we boarded?
I make a superhuman effort to control my emotions and
keep watching. Several minutes later I feel sure that the
police are checking documents for approximately one in
ten cars. That's a lot but it still gives us nine chances to get
through, doesn't it? The others around me are still just as
happy so I mustn't give any hint of my anxieties. Anyway,
it's time we got into the car and started waiting in line. I
call Zena.

"We did it, darling, we're going to catch the ferry! I'll
call you back in ten minutes when we've been through the
boarding gate."

"You be careful, ok? And call me as soon as you can."

Now I must just wait for Stéphan to call me back. He
sounded confident just now. There's nothing I can do
from here, anyway. It feels terrible but that's just the way

it is. Julia's sitting on the carpet in the living room laughing as she plays with her musical instruments—a xylophone, a tambourine . . . I usually come up with another idea pretty quickly because the cacophony is difficult to bear but the noise is welcome today, drowning out my thoughts.

While the car crawls toward the port, I give my passengers a few instructions.

"Be natural, ok, everyone smile! And we could have some music. Go ahead, Anas, find something on YouTube."

My young brother-in-law is delighted that he's allowed to fill the car with the latest hits from Avicii, DJ Snake, and Major Lazer.

Mayada is sitting next to me, flouting the usual rules of propriety because we're still playing the squeaky clean couple, and I've rolled down our windows so the police can see us clearly. On the other hand, having four passengers in the back—and three of them grown men—is a bit much. Despite the suffocating late August heat, I've asked my backseat passengers to keep their windows closed.

Julia turns to look at me every now and then, amazed that I'm not complaining. She tries even harder, thumping her xylophone with all her might. I can't really hear it. I'm fully focused on the screen of my phone. Waiting.

My clammy hands slip on the steering wheel. I try to look innocent, not too smiley, but not distant either. We crawl inexorably closer to the big steel gate that swallows cars one by one as their passage is authorized.

From afar, I study the policemen searching the trunks of cars, but mostly the officer standing a little way back, the one who intervenes occasionally to check people's papers.

When we're still five or six cars from the gate, I see him look over at us. Just for two or three seconds, no more, but he scrutinizes us intently. Then turns his attention back to vehicles closer to him.

Only one Ford left in front of us, and we've all fallen deathly silent inside my car.

The Ford goes through. I put the car into first gear to edge closer to the gate.

The policeman stares at us.

He walks toward me.

From the first step he takes, I get the picture.

It's all over.

Over.

My cell phone rings and I'm so startled I almost drop it. Julia says, "Daddy?" She's gotten used to seeing me on the phone with her father the whole time. But no, it's Sandra.

"I'm so sorry about this morning, Zena. This is really hard for my father, you know, you have to see it from his point of view. Look, I don't like thinking of you there all on your own while Stéphan's catching this ferry. I'll come over, ok?"

I mumble a vague "yes" and hang up quickly. I'm happy my sister-in-law's concerned about me but right now all I can think about is freeing up the line so Stéphan has no trouble getting a hold of me.

The policeman asks me for my documents, studies them at length, and hands them back. He tilts his chin toward the rear seat of the car.

"What about them?"

The words Zena kept repeating before I left come back to me in a flash: "If you get caught, say you don't know them." Impossible! There's no way I'm denying my loved ones.

"They don't have passports," I tell the policeman. "They lost them. But they're my family, they're my wife's parents."

Three more policemen—in uniform this time—have joined him. They stand behind him, arms crossed over their chests, legs spread, eyeing us menacingly. They think this is an open and shut case: I'm a people smuggler and these illegal immigrants are my clients.

"Documentation for the car!"

Sweat beads on my forehead. I can't seem to find my car registration document (Zena will discover later that when Julia was playing with my wallet she took it out and hid it under the sofa). The policeman turns to his coworkers.

"*And* the car's stolen."

Then he turns back to me and barks, "Step out of the vehicle!"

All six of us climb out of the car. One of the policemen sits at the wheel. The steel gate opens, he starts to drive through slowly and the uniformed policeman waves us after him, then they bring up the rear. Their hands hovering over their service pistols.

The police post is only a few hundred meters away. As soon as we're through the door the nightmare begins. The policemen push and prod us, yelling at us to remove shoelaces and belts—"Come on, faster, faster!" We're thrown into a cell and then called out one by one to have our fingerprints taken. Mayada faints and collapses onto the floor. Her father and I rush to pick her up but she can't stand. We don't yet know it, but she has a serious problem with her pancreas and this journey is especially punishing for her. My mother-in-law cries softly, terribly concerned for her daughter and clutching her arm, which is agony.

The policemen confer for a moment and eventually bring us a filthy old mattress and put it outside our cell.

"The women outside!" one of them snaps.

Wafaa and Mayada lie down on the mattress outside the locked cell where I sit disconsolately with Saif, Samer, and Anas.

There's a big problem, I just know it. Stéphan hasn't called back so I try to call him. But it hangs up immediately every time and then starts going straight to voicemail. He should have called me back by now. They've been arrested while they were boarding, I'm sure they have. I desperately want to cry, but I can't. Sandra's here, our daughters are playing together and we're drinking tea and chatting about how we'll arrange the house when my parents are living with us. When Sandra arrived she admitted that she'd had a fight with her father because she really didn't like the way he talked to me this morning. That gave me a moment's comfort. But I haven't told her I'm waiting for this call from Stéphan—I have this absurd feeling that voicing my concerns out loud could transform my fears into reality.

At about five in the afternoon I can't take it anymore. I break down and tell Sandra what's going on. Julia and Charlotte stare at me in alarm. My sister-in-law remains calm and tries to reassure me.

"I'm sure you'll hear from him soon."

———

We've been waiting for hours.

The temperature is over a hundred degrees in this cell, and I'm so thirsty. At first we tried to talk a bit but the heat and our fear soon floored us. Anas is sleeping, sitting propped against the cell wall. Samer is listless and utterly silent, holding his head in his hands. Saif is painfully dejected and keeps saying how ashamed he is to have put me in this situation. Not for a moment does he think of himself.

"Why did you come?" he asks from time to time. "You'll be in trouble now..."

I keep saying the same things over and over, reassuring words that I try to believe myself.

"It will all be fine, God is great, they won't kill us, don't worry, we'll be out soon..."

I regularly call out to the policemen who watch us from their office only a few meters away. I always ask for the same things: being allowed to call Zena, contact the French embassy, and ask for a lawyer. The answer is "no" every time, in defiance of the most fundamental rights and agreements regarding justice that are in force across Europe.

And then tiredness and despair win the day and we descend into silence. I've done everything to keep it at bay but I'm succumbing to my fear. It's so hot. What if there was a fire? Would anyone think about us in time, would we get out? If there's a full, French-style investigation this will go on for months! I'll lose my job and Zena doesn't have one. We've just taken out a huge loan to build our house. We've got a young daughter, shit, a very young daughter who needs us and now we're going to lose everything! I'm sinking, submerged in the horror film whose script I'm writing myself. But in all this darkness a series of luminous images come to me, as if part of my brain is standing guard to stop me from descending into madness. I remember the candlelit evenings when my grandmother read us the Gospels in Greek. She was very pious and had extraordinary mystic visions that she described to us after the readings. As a child I loved her descriptions of fantastical things and the wonders of ancient scripture. I've been thinking about her a lot since I've been in Greece. I can't explain this but I feel she's watching over me, from wherever she is.

Shortly before eight in the evening a policeman finally comes over to us with a document in Greek.

"You want food? Then sign this."

I refuse, without a moment's hesitation.

"I can't sign this, I don't know what it says."

"Just what happened, nothing else."

"But how can I be sure? I don't believe you."

"I'm the one who makes the decisions around here. Don't you get that?"

We're both getting heated. Alerted by our raised voices, another policeman—a younger man—intervenes. He takes his fellow officer to one side and they both disappear from view, then the younger officer returns with a sandwich and a bottle of water for each of us.

As I finish eating, the young man returns and talks to me through the bars.

"So, you speak Greek?"

"Yes, I have family here, my grandmother was Greek."

"And who are they, then?"

"They're my wife's family, her parents, her brother and sister, and her cousin."

He nods thoughtfully, then looks me right in the eye.

"Come, we're going to talk in my office."

He gets me to tell him my whole story, and all about Zena's parents, of course. He listens attentively and for the first time since our arrest I feel fully human again—I'm just a man sitting across from another man.

"So you see, they're my family," I say when I've finished explaining. "If your family was in their situation what would you do?"

"I do understand but I'm sure you know that there are people smugglers here every day, real ones taking advantage of people's misery to make money. It's my job to stop them."

"Ok but I'm definitely not a criminal! I'm not a criminal! Where are they, these criminals?"

"They're outside," he says simply, and I'm amazed by his honesty.

"Listen," he continues. "You'll have to appear before a judge tomorrow but by the evening you'll be out. We won't keep your family, they can try their chances again. But you be careful, if you're caught again, you're screwed. You'll go straight to prison. You must leave them to find their own way. And they can forget about sailing from Patras to get out of Greece, we've been closely monitoring this port for fifteen years because it's a hot spot for people smuggling."

I feel almost light-headed as he hits me with these harsh facts. I've failed, then, but that's not the worst of it. What will happen to Saif Eddine, Wafaa, and the others? How will they cope? How will they get out of Greece and not give up? My father-in-law will eventually snap and decide they should all go back to Syria. While I'm thinking about this, the young policeman suddenly does something extraordinary considering the circumstances: He turns his computer screen toward me.

"I'll show you. They'll have to go through Thessaloníki, then the Balkans. Look."

He does a quick Google search and clicks on a newspaper article explaining that Macedonia has just opened its border with Greece. In the summer of 2015, when thousands of migrants are traveling across Europe to get away from war, some countries have opted to look after their own interests and close their borders, but not Macedonia.

"There, that's the only way they can go, the only possible route."

He stands up.

"We're going to get you out of this police station, it's our closing time. Some of the officers will transfer you to another place for the night. We know your parents-in-law won't leave without their own children so the younger two can spend the night in a hotel if you've got the money for it."

"Of course, I'll give them the money."

I return to the cell with my mind full of new questions and fears but thankful for this conversation that has given me a relatively clear picture of what lies ahead. And whatever else happens, I'm glad Anas and Mayada can sleep in a hotel tonight. A few minutes after I get back to the cell, they come for us. I give Anas enough money to pay for a hotel room with Mayada. Before I climb into the van taking us to our accommodation, I'm allowed one telephone call. I choose to call Zena.

Julia and Charlotte have finished their dinner and Sandra has sat them down to watch a cartoon. Julia's far too young to understand it, but she's proud to be with her big cousin and that's enough to keep her happy. I suppose I should make something for Sandra and me to eat but I don't have the heart. And I'm not hungry either, obviously. The phone rings. It's Stéphan at last! His voice is expressionless and sounds very distant.

"We've been arrested."

I burst into tears.

"Don't worry, don't worry, my darling. Listen, this is important, I don't have the registration document for the car.

I need you to look for it and fax it to the number I'm about to give you as soon as possible."

"Ok, ok, but what's going to happen to you all?"

"We'll all get out tomorrow."

"Do you really believe that?"

"I'm sure of it. Fax over the document and everything will be fine. I promise."

I hear a rustling sound on the phone and the call is abruptly cut off.

Sandra breaks down and cries too when I tell her what Stéphan has just told me. I search all over the living room and eventually find the document under the sofa.

"We can't stay here," Sandra says. "This is unbearable. Get some things, we're all going back to my place for the night. There's a tobacco shop on my street that has a fax machine, we can send the fax first thing in the morning."

No one has told us where we're going. After a few minutes' drive we arrive outside a large, hangar-like building with a prefabricated sanitary block a few meters from the door.

"If you need the toilets, use them now," one of the policemen tells us.

Saif, Wafaa, Samer, and I take turns. The stench and filth are indescribable. Next, our handcuffs are removed and we're taken into the building. It looks like a gymnasium inside and is completely empty. We're immediately hit by an acrid smell of urine and excrement that catches at our throats. Strangely, we're alone. A policeman explains that we're lucky because otherwise they would have had to take Wafaa to a different hangar. It is only now that we realize we will be sleeping here, on the bare, grimy floor. I'm outraged, furious—is this Europe? Really? And is this how Europe treats people in custody? How can there be such total contempt for our dignity? I would never have believed that one of the world's top tourist destinations would inflict conditions like this on detainees, and people who have yet to be judged too! What upsets me most is seeing my elderly and already very strained parents-in-law being treated like cattle or criminals. But there's nothing I can do about it, nothing. My powerlessness is unendurable.

I settle myself on the floor and, with a big smile, Wafaa hands me the scarf she has around her neck, gesticulating for me to use it as a pillow. We have almost nothing left, but this almost nothing is shared. I wonder briefly at the close connection I have developed with Zena's parents. Until now there was always a restraint between us because of our cultures, the geographical distance between us, and the generation gap. We tended to feel a little awkward if the three of us ended up alone together without Zena. But since I arrived in Patras yesterday, that's in the past. I have become their son.

7

In court

We haven't slept a wink in this stinking hangar. I've spent the night calling myself a naive idiot and upbraiding myself for making all the wrong choices: I shouldn't have kept the rear windows of the car closed, we should have split into two groups, Zena's parents could have boarded on foot instead of in the car, and then we could all have slipped through unnoticed...I can hear Saif and Samer tossing and turning nearby, unable to get to sleep, and poor Wafaa moaning in pain every time she moves. After this sleepless night, the policemen come for us at eight o'clock. They handcuff us again and load us into the van that will take us to Patras's criminal courts in the pedestrian part of town. Three hundred meters short of our destination, the vehicle has to stop and we walk the rest of the way. I'll never forget the humiliation of those few minutes on foot—all those people watching us, staring at us! I'm dirty, handcuffed, with no belt or shoelaces...

We enter the building and are shown to the second floor. So far, only our fingerprints have been taken, back at the small police station, but now they start taking legal ID photos, face-forward and profile. Then we're split up: Samer, Wafaa, and Saif will be brought for an immediate trial within the day. Mayada and Anas are still at their hotel—oddly, they are not being prosecuted.

I, meanwhile, am taken before an examining magistrate, a woman of about fifty who does not respond to the nervous smile I give her. It is in this office, where there is also a court clerk and a uniformed policeman, that my handcuffs are finally removed. And at last, for the first time since my arrest, there is an interpreter present. She speaks French quite well, but has no knowledge of the law or legalese. I decide to play my "Greek-speaking" card again in an attempt to establish a connection with the judge: It seems to be working modestly and I think I can see her softening while we chat briefly about my Greek origins, her daughter's trip to France...but we very soon revert to the proceedings.

"Mr. Pélissier, would you like to have a lawyer?"

"Yes, of course."

"You should know that if you have a lawyer the proceedings will be extended by forty-eight hours."

"What? Well then, no, I don't want a lawyer. Anyway, I know the facts, I wanted to help my family who are in danger."

"Very well. So I suggest you plead guilty."

"I see."

"I shall list the evidence against you and the interpreter will relay it to you in French."

She lists the evidence and asks me if I accept it.

"Yes, those are the facts."

"Be careful, Mr. Pélissier, this is serious, we're talking about aiding and abetting the illegal movement of foreigners."

"I understand, but they're my family!"

"Well then, prove it."

"My family record book will prove we're related if you use it in conjunction with my father-in-law's driving license, but I don't have my record book—it's in my car, which has been impounded."

The judge turns to the uniformed officer and asks him to go look for the document. I see him roll his eyes before he leaves the office. The judge calls in another policeman, who puts on my handcuffs again: I must wait in the corridor until my family record book arrives at the courts. As for my father-in-law's driving license, we're lucky he still has it—it was in his pocket and not in the bag that was lost in the woods. It's a plasticized photocard, so it wasn't damaged at sea and is clear proof of his identity.

Less than an hour later I'm back before the judge. She peruses the family record book in front of me, tells me she acknowledges the family relationship, then says that I must now see the state prosecutor. I spend only a few minutes in the prosecutor's office, just long enough to run through the exact same information again, then I'm handcuffed and sent out to the corridor once more with the policeman and the interpreter, while the judge and prosecutor discuss my case.

"You could write a book about what's happened to you," the policeman says. "It's crazy!"

"Yes, I could. And you'd be in it!"

When I'm brought before the judge again she tells me my car will be kept in Patras because it was used in the offense. Next, she tells me there is a sum to pay—the interpreter calls it a fine: four to five thousand euros.

"But, your honor, I just don't have that sort of money! I'm the only breadwinner at home, my wife is a student, and we have a little girl of two…"

"I see, but how much money do you have with you?"

I search my pockets.

"I have three hundred euros on me."

"Perfect, let's go with three hundred euros!"

I can't believe my ears. Did I just haggle with a judge? In a democratic European country? Did I secure a more than 90 percent reduction on a fine?

The judge continues to explain procedural points that are beyond the scope of my Greek, so the interpreter relays that there will be a further hearing about my car in a year's time.

I emerge from the judge's office feeling that I just paid a reasonable fine. Yes, they're keeping my car and that's worth a lot of money (I bought it new less than two years ago), but I'm getting off lightly! And the judge definitely helped me out over the fine. The most important thing is I can now go home to France. That's great, I'm out of trouble, and the only thing I'm now worried about is my Syrian family.

The policeman does not handcuff me this time but takes me to the hearing room where other families in the same situation as mine are standing immediate trial. It is Saif, Wafaa, and Samer's turn to be heard. They're helped by an interpreter from Morocco whose dialect and accent are very different from the Arabic they speak: They barely understand every other sentence. In the space of a few minutes they are judged and condemned...but no penalty is handed down, no fine or prison sentence, and they are released on the spot.

The four of us are standing outside the courthouse, totally dazed by what's just happened. We're not yet completely free to go because the treasury where I have to pay my three-hundred-euro fine is already closed and will not reopen till the morning. I must go there before attempting to leave Greek soil.

But I now have two priorities: telling Zena we're free and getting Anas and Mayada to join us so we're all back together.

When I hear Stéphan's voice on the phone it sounds so different from yesterday that I'm flooded with hope. I listen as he explains that they're all free, just as he said they would be.

"So your parents were found guilty but there's no sentence, and I have to pay a fine of three hundred euros."

"Thank goodness. I'm so relieved. . . . One thing's clear, anyway, if the case can be dealt with in twenty-four hours and ends with a three-hundred-euro fine, then it's not such a big deal!"

How did we not guess that it wasn't really over?

8.

Coming back, alone

fter leaving the courts and being reunited with Anas and Mayada, we spend our last evening in Patras in a mood of slightly precarious happiness: It is genuine but fragile, threatened by the concerns for the future that we each harbor in our hearts. On the morning of August 25, it feels like I have the worst hangover of my life, which is grossly unfair because I haven't touched a drop of alcohol since arriving in Greece. But I'm so crushed, so disconsolate because of what I consider a personal failure, that my head feels as if it might explode at any moment. I thought I could help Saif, Wafaa, and the others, but I did them no good at all. My only victory is that my Syrian family won't attempt the Patras-Ancona crossing on an inflatable boat . . . but they will have to tackle the journey through the Balkans alone. So how can I be optimistic about their chances of reaching France without further injury, further scams, and further suffering?

When we say our goodbyes to board two different buses at the bus station in Patras, it tears me apart. My mother-in-law is crying. I try to stay strong, at least for Anas, who is making superhuman efforts to keep up a semblance of a smile.

"Ok, so it won't be long now, and we'll all be together again in France!" I say in what's meant to be a chirpy voice but sounds more like a croak.

Without my car, which is still being held by the Greek justice system, my return journey is quick: Zena has bought me a ticket on a direct flight from Athens to Toulouse. My wife has been with my sister for two days, so she comes to greet me at the airport with Sandra and the two little girls, Julia and Charlotte. In my wife's and daughter's arms, everything is erased from my mind for a few moments. Just in case the investigation took a long time, I prepared myself not to see them for months.

"We're lucky, we escaped the worst," Zena and I say to each other. Yes, but I wasn't supposed to come home alone.

As Sandra drives us back to our house, Zena and I discuss what will happen next. The way we see it, we need only retrieve the Dacia and my involvement in the whole business will be over. "In the next couple of weeks I'll call the embassy and try to get some information about the car. Maybe someone can explain what the procedure is and how long we'll have to wait," I say.

Our priority, though, is to see Zena's family safely to France. I have to go back to work once I'm home, and Zena spends a lot of time following their progress on the phone or on social media. She gives them all the long-distance help she can, reserving hotel rooms and searching for contacts and information, but despite all her efforts, she and I are only too aware of how powerless we are.

9

The challenge of crossing borders

ANAS'S STORY

Samer, my parents, my sister, and I were all together again with Stéphan for only a few hours before we had to say goodbye to this brave man who tried to save us. We did our best to appear confident, but there was nothing but sadness in the looks that passed between us.

After saying goodbye to Stéphan, we knew that we were now facing what we desperately wanted to avoid: crossing through the Balkans, especially Hungary. Social media sites are full of warnings from refugees about the despicable procedures that this country puts migrants through when they ask for asylum—and this behavior secures comfortable European grants for Hungary. Lies from the authorities, torture, arbitrary detention...these are all things we risk by traveling across this country. And if we do go against our better judgment and ask for asylum, we'll be "dublinned"* and therefore trapped: We would no longer be able to ask for asylum in France.

But there's no other solution. The policeman who talked to Stéphan clearly said that it was the only way, so we board a succession of buses to travel from Patras to Athens and then on to Thessaloniki. We get through Macedonia easily—their border is effectively open to Syrians, we were told the truth about that—and reach Serbia.

We spend a few days in the Serbian capital gathering together a group of refugees with whom to cross the border independently of any organized channels. The price for getting from Serbia to Germany with a people smuggler is prohibitive and we simply don't have the funds. We hear talk of some smugglers offering a much cheaper system that involves hiding in trucks transporting frozen goods. Suicide, in other words. And yet how many young Syrians have already been desperate enough to try that and have lost their lives in the process...

Our group gradually comes together over the course of a series of meetings. There are Syrians, Iraqis, and Afghans, all agreeing to travel from Belgrade to Hungary on foot. We set off one morning before dawn and only come within sight of the border as the sun is setting, having walked more than fifty kilometers. There are now two

---

* See the appendices for an explanation

possible routes for us to get into Hungary, and the group isn't unanimous. A minority want to take a particularly dark path that involves going through a forest and, more worryingly, across a river; they feel they will get through unnoticed in the darkness. The others, including my family, prefer a more brightly lit route through a forest and wheat fields. The river that has to be crossed on the former route is famously dangerous, and the first town that the "dark" path comes to has a reputation as a death trap for Syrians.

When we hear a plane flying low overhead we know it's all over. It is an official plane and we're stopped only a few kilometers after crossing the border. We hear later that the other group was also intercepted.

The policemen who stop us are brutal and very authoritarian. They keep saying we must register in Hungary but what exactly does that mean? Is this like in Greece? They take our names and assign each of us a number that they write on a wristband, then they tighten the bands around our wrists, deliberately hurting us as much as they can. They take no special precautions with my mother's broken arm and she screams in pain. Next, they bundle us onto a bus to take us to a migrant camp. I've heard about these places. I've even seen images filmed by refugees, but nothing has prepared me for the horror I find here. A policeman throws "provisions" at our feet: a half-liter bottle of water and a can of indeterminate meat three years past its use-by date. And that's all, for the five of us. In the two days we spend here we are given nothing else, no drinking water, no food, and no basic care. Of course there are no stores in the camp, and we are not allowed to leave. I'm getting used to being hungry, but I'm so thirsty...my throat's burning, I'm hot...when the police come near the fence we beg them to let us go back to Serbia. They snigger and taunt us cruelly.

"Wait, I'm not sure I get this, do you want to go to Serbia or Syria? You pronounce it so badly with your shitty little mouths!"

When they patrol the camp they strike out at people at random, kicking those who are sitting on the ground. They insult everyone, particularly mothers, because they know that's what hurts us most. To maintain the feeling that I have some purpose in what's happening to us, I use my phone to film evidence of the conditions we're kept in.

After two days we're led out of the camp in a group of about sixty refugees that is then split between two buses.

"Excuse me, where are we going?"

"Shut it, you Syrian shit!"

It turns out we're simply going to the police precinct. The bus drops us outside a small-town precinct to the north of Budapest. Our bus is the only one here because, we later learn, the policemen overseeing the passengers on the other bus offered to let them out for a fee...which they all accepted without a moment's hesitation. Sadly for us, the officers on our bus made no such offer. We're thrown into a cell, thirty of us packed in together. We're given no water or food and we're left to stew there for many long hours. At last an interpreter arrives and starts to explain what's going on. He is very elderly and the first thing he tells us is that he is Syrian, most likely to reassure us. He says we must each agree to have our fingerprints taken but we mustn't worry: That doesn't constitute a request for asylum, it's simply a way of registering that we're in Hungary. His deeply lined face shows no trace of emotion as he explains that anyone who refuses will stay in this cell for a very long time. In any event, we will all eventually be sent back to Serbia, but if we then try to tread on Hungarian soil again we'll go to prison for several years. Naturally, no one believes these lies. Some people in the cell shout out that they refuse to be fingerprinted. The interpreter looks at them intently.

"Well, you'll stay in here, then."

Others take out lighters, saying they'll burn their fingers so their prints can't be taken.

"If you want to get out of this cage," the interpreter repeats over and over again, "you have to agree to be fingerprinted."

I, meanwhile, am feeling worse by the minute. I have a high fever and need to lie down because I'm too weak to stand. I beg to be let out and then throw up violently into a bucket outside the cell before being shoved back inside.

Policemen come into the cell with the equipment for taking our fingerprints. Yes, it's going to be done right here, in this cage where we're crammed in like cattle in a truck heading for the abattoir. My parents look at each other. We don't have a choice, anyway. I hold out my hand but I'm shaking with fever so the print is blurred. The policemen yells right in my face and throws me to the floor.

"Try harder, sonny, this needs to be done right," the interpreter says, still just as impassive.

Other policemen stand in a group outside the cell, only meters from us. They stare and one of them laughs sneeringly as he gives us a one-finger salute.

After twenty-four hours in this cage, we're finally released at dawn. We're told we must return to the migrant camp and that we can make our own way there by catching a bus that leaves from outside the police precinct.

Mayada is the only one of us whose cell phone has any battery left. She calls Zena, tells her we've failed, we've been dublinned, we're stuck in Hungary and have to go back to the camp ... Zena tells Manal, and my two sisters search social media frantically for anyone who can get us out of Hungary. Of course, there's no way we're getting on that bus back to the camp—we make a run for it on foot. I'm so weak I have to lean on Samer the whole way, but luckily, after a few kilometers we come to a small town where there are taxis, and that's how we reach Budapest.

For the next five days we're stuck in the Hungarian capital until we can find a solution, a way out. I'm still very sick but cling to the thought that in France they will treat me, cure me, take care of me. Everything is expensive in this big beautiful tourist attraction of a city, and we spend our days in the streets or in parks, often in driving rain. Zena handles hotel bookings for us; the cheapest she can find of course, but we're aware how lucky we are not to be sleeping on the streets every night, as other Syrians do. Our research is difficult because we want to find a people smuggler we can really trust, one who will stay the course. There are very few in Hungary and, it goes without saying, the good ones are in high demand.

Then one day everything changes: The government officially announces, "All refugees are free to leave our country." We rush to the train station and buy tickets for Austria... and end up being rounded up with dozens of others who, like us, believed the government announcement. We're taken to the police precinct and my father tries hopelessly to explain that we were acting honestly.

"We're leaving the country, sir. Look, we have our train tickets."

A policeman snatches the tickets from him and takes us to an office where there's an interpreter. A man of average height, a little chubby, nicely dressed, almost elegant in fact, and with a likable, trustworthy face. The policeman speaks a few sentences of Hungarian to him and the interpreter explains that he has been given responsibility for explaining the procedure that lies in store for us. We're very surprised to see the policeman now leave the room.

"Listen," the interpreter continues, "I'm meant to be telling you that you're going back to the camp but I refuse to do that. I'm going to open this door for you and you can get out. But just don't get caught again."

We look at one another in amazement but don't have time to think—he's already opened the door out onto the street and is waving us out urgently.

"Come on, hurry! Get out, quickly!"

Is this man a hero, saving us out of sheer humanity? Or was the whole thing just a masquerade designed to confiscate our six-hundred-euro train tickets so they could sell them? I still wonder to this day. One thing is certain: In our whole long journey, Stéphan was the only person who helped us perfectly selflessly.

Laughing with surprise, we run to get away from the precinct and stop to catch our breaths after a few hundred meters. Incredible! We're free! But our euphoria is short-lived: Nothing's really changed. It's back to the hotel, back to looking for people smugglers. A couple of days later I finally establish firm contact with a man who seems to be for real. I tell my father about him and, after a few more WhatsApp exchanges, I'm ready to give the good news to the whole family.

"We're good, we have someone who'll get us out to-night!" I say. "He'll meet us this evening in a Turkish restaurant. I have the address."

Then I call Zena to let her know we'll be leaving Hun-gary tonight.

Our rendezvous at the restaurant is quick and busi-nesslike: We find the smuggler, he confirms the price he gave me before, my father pays him, and he takes us to a spot outside the restaurant where a car and driver are waiting to take us right away. We have a nasty surprise: The car is a disgustingly dirty wreck and the driver snoozing at the wheel reeks of alcohol.

I often think about that evening, still wondering how we could entrust our lives to this guy who was completely off his face and was meant to be driving us for 250 kilometers. I think it says a lot about the depths of our despair and our ability to ignore alarm bells. We'd already confronted so many fears, so much pain and sickness on our journey, and we'd been forced to override them in order to get anywhere, so our instinctive radars had stopped working.

The car has only been going a few minutes when the driver suddenly stops at a gas station, asks us to get out...and drives off! Unable to accept that he's abandoned us like this, we wait all night for him. By dawn it's obvious he won't come back. Mayada tells my father we must call Zena to let her know what's going on, but my father is beside himself, struggling to come to terms with this latest scam. His face has yellowed overnight, his eyes are bloodshot, and he's stopped talking. So Mimo calls Zena herself and tells her about this new disaster. My poor sister, who's doing everything she can to help us from France, is devastated. And I feel so guilty...after all, I was the one who found this contact, and what we paid him has cleaned us out, we have nothing left to pay for the trip with another smuggler.

Still, we pull ourselves together quickly. The people smuggler will just have to pay us back, that's all there is to it! This becomes an obsession: We harass him on social media and post messages describing what happened to us so no more refugees will use him until he gives us our money back.

In the end, he agrees to meet us. Of course, he shows up with two huge men built like tanks and these thugs stand on either side of him while he talks to my father. Samer and I think they're going to beat up my father. We edge closer, ready to pounce, two skinny, sickly seventeen-year-olds who've only ever fought other schoolboys.

My father asks for his money but the smuggler says he won't pay us back.

"I'll organize another ride for you but with a good driver this time. There's no way I'll give you your money back so you can go give it to another dealer, that would be an insult to me!"

It's now clear that the man's only concern is his reputation. If we go to another smuggler, word would quickly get around about how he treated us and that would put off other customers. Luckily, we've heard that the small town of Sopron, close to the Austro-Hungarian border, is a good place for relatively easy border crossings without a people smuggler. So my father gamely says that we need the money back because we're going to undertake the journey alone, via Sopron, rather than giving it to another dealer. This lie is our last hope but, unbelievably, it works: The man returns all the money to my father!

Back to square one: We now need to find a good people smuggler to get us out of this wretched country. We get in touch with all our contacts, even down to people we met in Greece, and finally—*finally*—we find the right person. So right, in fact, that we have to wait till he has room for us, but in the end the rendezvous is set up in the same Turkish restaurant where we met the other man. After checking that our crook won't be there this evening, we sit down for our last meal in Hungary: rice with kidney beans followed by rice pudding with raspberries and lots of sugar. As she finishes this delicious desert, Mayada gives a big smile.

"That was so good it's bound to bring us luck tonight!" she says.

Our smuggler arrives. Dark hair, long beard, and uncovered head; he's under thirty and wearing a Batman T-shirt. He doesn't talk much but counts out the money that my father hands him in an envelope: 2,500 euros. His face lights up.

"Perfect, you're leaving right now. I'll take you to the car."

We can't believe our eyes when we get there. In fact, there are two cars, because our smuggler wants no more than four passengers per vehicle, one in the front passenger seat and three in the back. They're both big, brand-new German sedans, a Mercedes and a BMW. I immediately feel safe...but there are five of us: one of us will have to travel in the other car with three men we don't know. My father turns to Samer.

"You will travel in the other car," he says.

"But I'm frightened, I don't want to."

"Don't worry, Samer," I say. "I'm sure everything will be fine."

"I don't know..."

"Listen, it's ok, I'll go instead of you, you can stay with my parents and Mimo."

"Really? Well then, no, if you really trust them, I'll go."

The driver of the car I get into with my parents is very attentive. He introduces himself, says that he's Hungarian and a Muslim, and attaches a strand of Misbaha prayer beads to the rearview mirror. He reassures us that Samer will be fine, saying that the BMW will follow right behind us, especially because the other driver doesn't know the minor roads as well as he does, and that's the route to take to avoid being spotted. He even offers us a glass of orange juice and says he'll stop along the way as soon as anyone needs a break.

He's not just obliging, he's also very clever. We're hurtling along a little-used road when we spot flashing blue lights up ahead: There's been an accident and the emergency services are on the scene. Our driver doesn't miss a beat. He tells us to huddle on the floor of the car so we can't be seen and stops very close to the accident. He gets out and walks right over to the police. We hold our breaths as we watch him talk to them briefly—were we right to trust him?—then he runs back to the car and we set off again with the BMW still behind us.

"I asked if there was anything I could do to help, so they just told me to get out of the way," he says, winking at me in the rearview mirror.

A couple of hours later he suddenly says, "You see over there, that's the Austrian police. I won't go any farther, but if you head left here, you'll find taxis. Out you get, and run!"

He's absolutely right, the GPS on our phones confirms that we've reached Austria. And then there really are taxis less than a kilometer away. We set off for Vienna with a driver who doesn't ask us a single question.

After the strain of the last few weeks, we don't want to waste another second. It's still the dead of night but we head for the main train station in Vienna, where huge Red Cross banners lead us to a reception area under a white tent. Two kindly and very smiley men greet us when we walk in. They're wearing Red Cross vests and tell us that they're Egyptian and they're here to help refugees like us. I don't know if this is what they expected, but we tell them everything from when we left Damascus to arriving here, often all talking at once. They listen attentively, never asking us to cut things short. When we finally stop talking, we're breathless.

"There are no trains at this time of night," they tell us. "You can't leave until the morning."

"But we hardly have any money left, we can't go to a hotel here, it'll be too expensive."

"Don't worry, we can take care of you, we have a big center nearby."

We have a brief discussion and decide to trust them, and one of them takes us to the Red Cross center. It starts really badly: A group of volunteers makes a note of our names and gives us wristbands with numbers on them, telling us that we must wear them the whole time we're in the center. I brace myself, I have such vivid memories of the exact same sort of wristband that was forced onto me in Hungary. I tell the volunteers how I'm feeling and they reassure me, very gently and kindly. We're given a few provisions: water, apples, sardines, tuna—and none of it out of date! Then we settle down for the night in this center, which is a little like a hospital with rows of beds lining long corridors as far as the eye can see.

The next morning we meet the two Egyptians outside the station. They're surrounded by a crowd of refugees.

"Listen up, everyone! Special trains have been chartered for refugees, you can travel to Germany for free."

This announcement is greeted with whoops of joy. The five of us fall into one another's arms. Our destination is getting closer at last, and fast! My mother and sister embark on happy, animated conversations with other Syrians around us, describing our experiences and listening to theirs. Most of the other refugees will end their journey in Germany, that's where they intend to ask for asylum. Others will continue to the Netherlands. We are the only group wanting to settle in France.

When we reach Munich station, I gaze in disbelief at the surreal scene before me. Hundreds of Germans are waving placards with the word "Welcome!" in German and Arabic. Some have teddy bears to give to refugee children, but even this can't bring a smile to my face because I've noticed that there are also policemen on the platform, dozens of them. And that surely can't be a good sign. But this isn't Hungary and I realize that the policemen treat us with respect, asking if anyone needs any kind of urgent help, before showing us to a line of buses waiting by the station. One of them uses a megaphone to make an announcement in several languages.

"We will take you to a camp near Berlin and you will spend a week or two there. Then you will be brought for immediate trial and if you want to leave Germany, you must explain that you're not seeking asylum here but in another country. Then you'll be free to travel to your chosen destination."

I climb onto the bus alongside my family with a heavy heart—going to Berlin takes us farther from Paris, and I definitely don't want to spend two more weeks in a migrant camp. During the journey, my father comes to see each of us individually and whispers something in our ears…and as soon as we've retrieved our baggage from the hold when we reach the camp, we run away as quickly as we can.

We're terrified that we'll be followed but no one sets off on in pursuit. Once we're a reasonable distance from the camp, we stop to catch our breaths and assess the situation. A few minutes' research on our phones is all it takes to work out that it should be quite easy to get to France: There's a high-speed train from Berlin to Luxembourg and another from Luxembourg to the Gare de l'Est in Paris. We hurry through the freezing cold city of Berlin to the main station. It's September 6, but the ground even feels icy in places. We have only summer clothes, and not a single sweater between us. I'm not as cold as the rest of my family because of my fever, which still won't drop. When we reach the station, my father takes us into a pharmacy where the pharmacist—moved by the state that I'm in and by my mother's swollen, bruised arm—agrees to sell us a powerful painkiller, tramadol, without a prescription.

We board the InterCity Express train for Luxembourg and I find myself sitting opposite an older lady who smiles at me with genuine kindness. The time comes for the train to leave but we don't move and after a few minutes there's an announcement in several languages saying that, due to a technical problem, our train cannot leave and we will have to catch the next one.

"That's incredible!" the lady says in English. "I've been taking this train regularly for fifteen years and I've never known it to have a problem."

In the delirium of fever, these simple words throw me into a state of absolute torment. I must bring bad luck, it's my fault the train's not going... But an hour later we're on a moving train at last and I succumb to fitful sleep punctuated by jolts of wakefulness when I go over and over the idea that I don't want to die before seeing my sisters Zena and Manal again, so I must keep going.

And then out of nowhere Mayada is shaking me, saying, "Anas, we're here, we're in Paris!"

I'm completely dazed and realize I have no recollection of changing trains in Luxembourg.

Manal and Khaled are waiting for us at the end of the platform. They hug us so tightly I think I might break, but it's wonderful. Manal takes a step back and looks me up and down. My weight has dropped to 136 pounds, my beard has grown because I had no way to shave, and I'm ashen from the fever. She starts to cry, and so do I. All those days filled with anxiety, all those sleepless nights of terror, the abuse, the hours in the rain or scorching sun with no shelter—it's all over.

We're home and dry at last. We have shelter at last. In France at last. Safe.

I'm happy in France now. I go to school here, I have friends and life's treating me well. There's only one thing that makes me sad: I can never go back to Syria, ever. Because as a political refugee, I can travel anywhere in the world except my native country, even for a few days. My grandmother will die, and I won't have seen her again, I know that. She'll be buried without us. And that hurts.

10

(Re)united

It's Sunday September 6, 2015, and—as we often do on a Sunday—we're having lunch with Stéphan's parents. Julia is on my lap, picking at the food on my plate. She's already had her own lunch, but she is only two, after all! I'm not hungry, though, and she's the one savoring the roast potatoes my mother-in-law has served me. This is a special day: I know that my parents, my brother and sister, and Samer are on a train, on their way from Berlin. They've kept me up-to-date on an almost hourly basis. I'm feverish with excitement. Conversation buzzes around me: Stéphan and his parents are talking about my family's arrival. Everyone's happy, but I'm withdrawn, almost silent. The journey that my family has been on since they left Damascus has involved countless obstacles, *so much suffering, and so many dead ends...I can't possibly celebrate until I'm sure they're safely on French soil.*

My phone rings at last. It's Mimo.

"We did it! I'm not lying to you, Zena, our train's pulling into the station, we're in France! We're in Paris!"

I burst out laughing and crying in the same breath. At last! After this journey of constant ordeals, they made it! When I hang up I don't need to explain what's going on: Everyone knows. My father-in-law, Claude, stands up.

"I'm going to get some champagne, I think that's what's needed!"

I hug my daughter to me, overwhelmed with emotion, kissing her little head and getting lost in the smell of her. To think I was worried this moment of relief might never come. We're finally done with the years of anxiety when we knew they were in danger in a war zone, and the weeks of terror, worrying that the worst has happened to them as they tried to get away. I have an irrepressible urge to jump up and set off to Paris to fetch them immediately. But I know that my sister Manal is there to greet them, and she'll take care of them until Stéphan and I go to pick them up next weekend.

Stéphan comes over and puts his arms around Julia and me. That's when I truly succumb to my tears, and he holds me all the more tightly. After this moment shared between the three of us, I look up and smile at Marianne and Claude; he is now filling our champagne flutes and is clearly very moved himself. After all the tension and fear, it means a lot to me that I'm sharing this boundless joy with my parents-in-law.

Manal waits till everyone is in bed before calling me.

"So, how are they?" I ask.

"Well, it was high time they got here, they're exhausted. They hardly ate anything, even the boys, they just wanted to wash and go to bed, so I didn't insist."

"Apart from being tired, though, are they ok?"

"They need to see a doctor, especially Mom with her arm, obviously. I'll take them to the emergency room first thing in the morning."

"Keep me in the loop, won't you?"

"Of course I will. But I warn you, Zena, they've really changed, you'll have a shock when you see them on Saturday."

"I know. I'm so happy that they're with you, thank God. Take good care of them."

The very next morning, Manal and Khaled take my parents, Mimo, Anas, and Samer to the emergency room at a hospital in Orléans. But, because they have no form of ID or any insurance, it's a real obstacle course. The care they get is determined by the goodwill of the hospital staff. Manal assures me that all the health-care workers they meet are attentive and kind. But only my mother is seen to immediately, and this is due to her urgent need for treatment. Once she has been x-rayed, her arm is finally put in plaster. Despite their requests, there are no examinations or treatments offered to my father, my sister, Samer, or Anas: Their problems are not sufficiently visible. Manal buys over-the-counter drugs to alleviate Samer and Mayada's pain, bring down Anas's temperature, and tend to my father's cuts and abrasions.

Of course, sleeping in a real bed every night and sharing in happy family meals will also help them recuperate.

Stéphan hasn't taken any time off work so we must wait till the weekend to join them. In the meantime, I call them one at a time every day. Just to hear their voices, to ask my father what he's had to eat, and my mother whether she slept well. And although I still miss them, I'm finally recovering my appetite, my own ability to sleep, and my smile. I almost can't believe it: I've stopped worrying every time the phone rings that it will bring news of some crisis, and I'm even getting back into the habit of switching it off when I go to bed—I don't think I've done that for three years. It's as if I've finally put down a backpack full of concrete blocks that I've been carrying around for months...

To kill the time I finally allow myself to get everything ready for them at home. Out of superstition, I didn't want to do much shopping or make too many arrangements until they were in France. Ever since my father's decision to leave Syria, it's been agreed that they would all come to live with us. As it stands, there are just three of us in our four-bedroom house in Albi, whereas Manal and Khaled have four children and less space. And so, the following Saturday, Stéphan and I settle little Julia into the minibus we've hired for the occasion and we set off for Orléans. I've tried my best to explain to her what's going on. I'm not sure she fully understands but she's very aware that Stéphan and I have been filled with euphoria and incredulous excitement the last few days. "Something wonderful's going to happen to Mommy and Daddy. I don't exactly know what, but it looks like it's gonna be amazing!"

Halfway to Orléans, we stop to pick up a TV crew and Ghislaine Buffard, a director whom Manal and Khaled met when they came to France in 2014. She has already made a report about the two of them and is now filming another as part of her work documenting refugees for the production company 416 Prod. So she wants to be with us for our family reunion. When Manal mentioned this to me, I wasn't sure at first, uncomfortable with the idea of a camera being around for an intimate moment that I've been looking forward to so much. But I thought a lot about how significantly media coverage helped Manal; if it could also help my parents, I shouldn't be hesitating. And I must also acknowledge that Ghislaine is extremely considerate, doing everything she can to be discreet and not hijack the event: She's happy to film us as we all meet up outside the house and then slip away to leave us alone. Once inside Manal's house, we can finally have the reunion I've envisioned in my daydreams.

I don't know how long I hug my parents, little sister, and little brother. We've waited a lifetime for this! I wish this moment could go on forever. When I let go of them, finally convinced that they really are here, I study them from every angle. Even though Manal warned me, I'm horrified to see how my parents have changed physically. I last saw them in June in Beirut, for a get-together we've had every year since our marriage, and I'm shocked by how much they've aged. They're both very thin and their sunken cheeks are a painful reminder of the countless days when they had nothing to eat. And if their happiness comes shining through, it's only in their exhausted eyes. I try to catch Manal's eye as she serves tea and baklava, and she nods without a word: She knows what I'm thinking. I fight to hold back the tears I can feel welling up; it really wouldn't be right for me to cry when they all have such huge smiles. It's obvious how happy they are to be here. And when I ask them about the ordeals they've been through since they left Damascus, they underplay everything as if it is all far removed from them, almost as if they're telling someone else's story. Still, I can't help flinching just at the mention of nights spent wandering in search of a hotel that might finally agree to take them, the violence they experienced at the hands of the police, the boat that went down in the middle of the night, and could have cost them their lives...Looking back, I think my parents' calm attitudes and their smiles derived more from their fierce determination to be parents to their children—to be proud, worthy, invincible—than the distance that victims can somehow establish between themselves and their traumatic experiences.

As for Julia, she's only met them twice, but she's thrilled to be part of such a big family reunion! With all the confidence of a two-year-old, she races from one person to another, sits on her grandmother's knee for a moment, trots off to kiss Uncle Anas, and comes back to demand a cuddle from her grandfather. My head's spinning: What would be a commonplace family gathering for millions of people feels totally surreal to me. For weeks I've been picturing the worst, conjuring *mental images of my parents on the inflatable boat, Anas in custody, Mayada in the camp in Hungary, and Samer in the sedan on the way to Austria... But I never dared dream of this simple living room where, amid the honey and pistachio smell of pastries, my little daughter punctuates our conversations with her musical laugh.*

I have work on Monday so the hours seem to be flying by: We need to be back on the road early on Sunday morning to get home to Albi. Julia laughs uproariously as all eight of us climb into the minibus. She's right, it's a happy sort of mayhem.

I try not to show Zena how relieved I am that her family is now safely in France because that relief is in direct proportion to the anxiety that's haunted me ever since I left the five of them in Patras. Not just left, I feel I abandoned them. Either way, I'm enjoying this wonderful new feeling of weightlessness. It's great, the nightmare's over.

We now have two priorities: their ID papers and their health. For several months, Zena will devote all her time and energy to helping them with these. Her family has now been in France for a week, but legally they don't exist, and that is what we start with first thing on Monday morning. Five minutes before it opens, we're outside Albi's local administrative offices. Zena knows the place well because she needs to come here every year to renew her residence permit. This isn't a complicated exercise in itself, but it's very tedious. She must be armed with all sorts of documents and be very careful about timing—the application for renewal must be submitted two months before the present permit expires, and the new permit is allocated at a meeting held three months after the previous one has expired. In the meantime a simple receipt for the ongoing application acts as proof of the applicant's legitimacy.

In 2013 I went with my wife when she submitted her renewal application: Julia was very young and Zena couldn't leave her with anyone. The three of us arrived at precisely nine o'clock in the morning but were far from the first people there. Several families were milling outside the doors well before opening time to be sure they would be seen. That's right: Curiously, the department handling foreigners was the only one in the whole building that was open just in the morning. While Zena looked in vain for somewhere to sit down with Julia in her arms, I took a ticket and studied the crowd of people in the small waiting room. At the time there were very few who appeared to be from the Middle East, but there were Africans and Eastern Europeans. Teenagers, children, the elderly, men and women; clearly, whole families had come to go through the process. There were three counters facing the waiting room but only one was open, and Zena told me it was always like this. Julia was restless and started crying. It was a long time till our number would be called, so Zena went off for a walk with her in the stroller.

I watched the local government officer manning the single desk. When she took the papers handed to her by applicants, she never looked up at them, just mumbled terse replies and woe betide anyone who hadn't yet fully mastered the French language and asked her to repeat herself: She strenuously demonstrated her exasperation with sighs or even icily contemptuous comments. I was overcome with anger. What did she think? That these people were here for the fun of it, or just to annoy her? What did it cost to smile, to be patient and welcoming to people who were destitute and in distress? When Zena returned with Julia she reassured me that some of the staff were far more amenable, but now I was the one who needed to go out for a walk to calm down. I didn't want to compromise my wife's case so I took it upon myself to keep quiet when, at about 11:30, it was finally our turn.

So on this Monday morning in September 2015, I have not come to the office with very positive expectations. It's 8:50 and there are already around thirty people outside the door. By 9:30 there are upwards of sixty of us in the department's small waiting room. The crowd is very different from the one I remember, and, listening to people's conversations, Zena confirms what I'm thinking.

"It seems like there are quite a few Syrians here."

After a two-hour wait, the Al Khatib family is called at last. We are greeted by the same icy woman as in 2013. I keep my mouth shut and let Zena do the talking.

"Good morning, I'm here with my family. They've just arrived in France but they have no papers and are going to ask for refugee status."

"Oh, we don't do that here anymore, we don't handle requests for asylum. You need to go to Toulouse, they have the software. I'll arrange a meeting for you."

She prints out a slip with the time of our meeting at the offices in Toulouse in two weeks.

"And will we need to take any particular documents with us?"

"Listen, I don't have time to go into the details for you, there are people waiting! They'll tell you everything when you get there."

Saif Eddine and Wafaa are very disappointed.

"Is that it then? We have no status for another two weeks?"

My father-in-law was mayor of his neighborhood and the local registrar, so he is humiliated to know he is on French soil illegally. Zena's whole family can't wait to go to Toulouse where they will be registered officially. I, meanwhile, have only been able to take the morning off and it's not until dinner that Zena tells me about the rest of their day.

Neither of us knows much about the status and rights of refugees but Zena refuses to sit and do nothing until the meeting in Toulouse. She does some research on social media and eventually lands on a page about Terry Hugot, a woman from Albi who campaigns for Amnesty International. Zena knows her; Terry teaches English at the University of the Third Age, and Zena has been to several of her seminars. After a brief exchange of messages, Zena calls Terry, who gives her some valuable information: Whatever their status, foreigners can go to the free clinic at Albi hospital for treatment. She also recommends that Zena contact a social worker as soon as possible to get a clear idea of her family's rights.

The next day Zena takes Saif Eddine, Wafaa, Mayada, Anas, and Samer to the clinic in the hopes of securing an appointment for each of them. The receptionist is all smiles.

"I'd be very happy to arrange appointments for you but the doctor's free now, she can see you right away if you like."

Zena's delighted, and moments later Dr. Isabelle R. arrives. Her dark blonde bob frames a warm smile that puts everyone at ease. She takes the time to listen to their stories, then describes the medical assessments she will carry out for each of them, explaining that, depending on the outcome of these assessments, some of them may then go on to have further tests. When Zena relates this conversation to me, she is clearly still moved by how gentle and humane the doctor was, by her ability to explain calmly and reassuringly. Bearing in mind the countries through which they have traveled and the conditions of their journey, Dr. R. gives them each a Mantoux test. This involves an injection of fluid that produces a skin rash if the person is a tuberculosis carrier. They are also given chest x-rays, a full range of blood tests, and a number of vaccinations. The doctor then takes Wafaa into her office to examine her—she's noticed the pitiful state of my mother-in-law's plaster. Rather than respecting advice from the doctor in Orléans or listening to Manal, Wafaa has continued to wash clothes by hand and do the cooking and housework as soon as her daughter's back is turned. The waterlogged plaster is worse than useless.

"I was really scolded!" Wafaa tells me with an impish smile. "The doctor told me I'll need an operation if I don't look after it this time. I absolutely promise I won't get the new plaster wet."

Zena and I both warn her we'll be watching her and this makes her laugh. Zena confides to me separately that the doctor asked her to keep an eye on her mother because her blood pressure is very low. She's exhausted from the journey, and yet she's always smiling, well turned-out, busy in the kitchen, going to endless trouble to cook dishes that I love. She may not allow herself to express any anger or sadness but has clearly been deeply affected by what they endured on their journey. The brush with death on that makeshift boat was a terrible shock, but she can't bring herself to talk about it. A few days after their arrival she asked me whether she could use my computer to go onto Facebook (something she hadn't yet done since she'd been in France), and some time later I found her there in tears. She'd just seen a photo of little Alan Kurdi, the three-year-old boy found dead on a Turkish beach in early September. Images of his tiny body lying facedown in the sand went viral just as Wafaa reached France. I'd never seen my mother-in-law cry like this. Zena took her mother in her arms and let her own tears flow too. They wept as much for the horror that Wafaa experienced firsthand that night on the sea between Turkey and Greece as for the tragedies of all the little Alans in the world whose parents—out of love or despair—take them on improbable boats in an attempt to get them away from bombings.*

Over that week Zena goes with her family to the free clinic every day for each of them to receive the treatment he or she needs. Saif Eddine's fasting blood glucose levels are very high and he has bruises and slow-to-heal abrasions all over his body. Isabelle R. diagnoses severe diabetes, and to ensure that his illness is handled as effectively as possible, she refers him to a diabetologist

---

* According to the International Organization for Migration (an intergovernmental organization related to the United Nations), more than 17,000 people died in the Mediterranean between 2014 and 2018 while trying to reach Europe.

and a cardiologist in the hospital. Zena is very touched that the doctor personally makes calls to secure swift appointments with her colleagues, not to mention that—as part of the care package provided by the free clinic—these consultations will also be free. As far as medication is concerned, Dr. R. and her colleagues always try to prescribe drugs available at the hospital's pharmacy, which means we have nothing to pay. If this isn't possible, Zena and I cover the cost.

The doctor's main advice for Samer, Anas, and Mayada is to get plenty of rest and eat regular meals to regain weight. Anas needs a course of antibiotics: The high fever he has had almost nonstop since Hungary is due to an infection that has really worn him down and that his body can't fight alone. Meanwhile, Mayada still has abdominal pains (she was already in pain back in Syria and had her appendix removed, but to no effect), and the doctor prescribes painkillers for her.

We'll never forget this extraordinary woman, this exceptional doctor. Thanks to the treatments she administered, and thanks also to her attentiveness and gentleness, she healed the wounds that the journey from Damascus inflicted on Saif, Wafaa, and the children. When they had only just arrived in France and their future was so uncertain, she embodied the security that my country can and should give them.

———

A few days after Zena's family has moved in with us, my parents invite all eight of us for lunch at their house so that they can all meet. This is a very symbolic occasion for Zena and me because we weren't able to arrange for them to meet before we were married. My father knows from previous conversations with me that Saif Eddine was a local mayor in Syria, and, while we're having our aperitifs, he surprises me by offering my father-in-law his red, white, and blue sash! He says a few words that Zena translates:

"Saif Eddine, I would like to welcome you, *we* would like to welcome you to France. With this sash I hope you'll feel that our whole country is proud to be a home to you when your own is so full of suffering."

Saif shakes my father's hand for a long time, clearly very moved. Zena and I are overwhelmed by this gesture. Beyond their differences of language and culture, these two patriarchs have always striven to be exemplary citizens and proud holders of their elected positions, as well as responsible fathers doing the best for their families. Our mothers immediately establish a wonderful rapport, and this doesn't surprise us because we've always thought them so similar: gentle, kind, reserved, and always thinking of others before themselves.

Sandra and my mother have prepared a meal with Greek and French flavors, starting with a mezze of egg-plant dip, tzatziki, fried calamari, and tomato and feta salad, followed by Basquaise chicken. Samer and Anas eat like horses and nothing could make my mother happier. Wafaa asks to see the recipes, and Zena follows the two grandmothers off into the kitchen. When she comes back her cheeks are flushed with happiness:

"They're managing to talk to each other, I don't really get how, but anyway they just can't stop laughing!"

Between two appointments at the clinic during their first week with us, Zena looks into Samer and Anas's education. Terry Hugot told her that they are eligible to attend school, but it isn't compulsory because they're over sixteen. Either way, the first step is to have them sit for the CASNAV tests to evaluate their abilities in French and mathematics. For now, their mastery of French is far too limited for them to attend French-speaking school, but their files have been sent out to all the high schools in and around Albi, so Zena says we just need to keep our fingers crossed.

It's only been a week since they moved in, and I already can't think how we lived without them. We settle into a routine very quickly, all eight of us happy together. My parents-in-law are in one of our guest bedrooms and Mayada the other, while Samer and Anas sleep in the living room. We all meet up every morning over breakfast to enjoy a variety of savory dishes that Wafaa, Mimo, and

Zena take pleasure in preparing: omelets, hummus, marinated olives, *labneh*—the Middle Eastern flavors take me right back to my grandmother's house, and a number of forgotten memories are brought back to me through my taste buds. I call my mother regularly to launch into conversations that begin, "And do you remember when...," which is a joy for both of us. Over dinner in the evenings, Zena and her parents tell me about their days while Julia tastes every dish, sitting on a different person's lap each time. She's crazy for hummus on sliced bread—not a very traditional combination but who cares!

Caught up in the emergency of taking in her family, Zena and I never really considered how we would all get along together. Well, it all turns out to be remarkably easy and cheerful. Yes, we have to be careful with budgeting, but Zena and I are happy to surrender some excesses so that everyone under our roof has clothes and plenty to eat. Yes, the house is full and there are sometimes traffic jams in the bathrooms, so Anas and I have gotten into the habit of waking very early each morning, taking turns to shower, and then sharing the sink to shave side by side like brothers while listening to rap music on his phone—but not too loud because some people are still asleep! In my mental picture of us as a family we're all together around a big table of food, in a room full of laughter. My daughter is radiant, like a little princess surrounded by her courtiers. And Zena... even tired at the end of busy, complicated days, I've never seen her so happy. She admits that she wouldn't allow herself to be happy here when she knew they were in danger over there. She thought about them all the time, about the risks they were running first in Syria and then on their journey. It's over! It's over...

11.

Foreigners

The following week the social worker who Zena contacted on Terry Hugot's advice comes to our house to evaluate the situation, and Zena is relieved to have someone to give her some guidance.

"I do all this running around and research," she confides in me, "but I'm always worried something could be passing me by or I might be doing some harm."

Over a cup of tea, Sibylle P. listens to the Al Khalib family's accounts of their journey and then starts to examine the papers that each member has filled in at Albi's administrative offices, along with the results of the boys' CASNAV tests.

"Tell me, Mrs. Pélissier," she says, "am I right in thinking Samer isn't your brother?"

"Yes, that's right, he's my cousin."

"So he has no legal guardian here in France?"

"No..."

Zena feels a dark pit open up inside her stomach. She knows instantly, she admits to me later. She knows even before the social worker says anything more.

"Unfortunately, he can't stay with you. He's a minor and you're not his parents."

"But we're the only relations he has in France."

"I understand but it's the law. I'll help you get him into a school, just as I will with Anas, but I'll also contact shelters for unaccompanied minors to find him a place in the area. The director of whichever shelter has room for him will then be responsible for Samer's asylum application."

It takes all Zena's strength to hold back her tears. Samer has heard his name and seen Sibylle P. looking at him. He doesn't understand what she's saying and is studying Zena's face—she can't leave him in suspense.

"Can I have a moment, please. I need to translate for Samer."

When Zena has finished explaining what's going on, Samer sits there speechless for a moment and then retreats, devastated, to take refuge with Anas in Julia's room.

The social worker stands up.

"I understand how difficult this is, I'll leave you together for a moment. I need to call the school that I think will best meet Anas and Samer's needs."

Wafaa goes to fetch the two boys and does her best to console Samer, who feels rejected and abandoned. His father walked out on him and his mother just as he was taking his first steps; he has fled his country, leaving behind his mother with no idea when he'll see her again; we are all the family he has and now he's to be dragged away. Anas is fighting back tears too. He has always been very close to his cousin, but they have become brothers over the course of their shared ordeals. Saif is quiet, somber: He feels he is being asked to abandon someone he promised to look after. He puts his hands on Samer's shoulders.

"Samer, I promise you, we'll always be here for you. Let's wait till we know what sort of place you're offered in a shelter, then we'll see."

When the social worker knocks on the door to join us again, calm has been restored, at least to outward appearances. Sibylle P. smiles at Anas and Samer, then turns to Zena.

"You can give them some good news: They'll be in the same class together at high school from next Monday!"

Zena can't get over it, it's incredible. The two boys have very limited French for now but they have places in the FLE—French as a foreign language—tenth grade at the Toulouse-Lautrec High School right here in Albi, the only school for miles around to take in non-French speakers like this. Samer and Anas were both in eleventh grade in Syria, but this FLE class will mean they have time to become comfortably fluent in French. Knowing that they will be together in school at least is some comfort to Samer and Anas, and reassures Zena and her parents.

Sibylle P. goes over our household income with Zena.

"You have only one salary coming in, that's tricky. I don't know if you know this but your parents and sister could claim financial support, at least once they're properly registered in Toulouse."

"Well, we have heard about that," Zena says, "but how does it work?"

"It's called ATA* and it's means-tested financial assistance for adult foreigners. So Samer and Anas are not eligible for it because they're under eighteen. And the hitch is that the only way this allowance can be paid is by bank transfer into the beneficiary's account, which means the three of them will need to open accounts at La Banque Postale, because that's the only one that offers accounts to foreigners. I might as well warn you that they won't have checkbooks or credit cards. They'll each receive around three hundred euros a month."

Zena calls me as soon as the social worker has left to let me know about Samer and the ATA—heartache on the one hand, and on the other a piece of positive news for my parents-in-law, who won't feel so dependent on us. There's never a dull day for our family!

---

* "Allocation temporaire d'attente," a temporary allowance that was discontinued in 2017

By the end of the week, the director of a children's home in Castres has contacted Zena. They have a place for Samer and he must go as soon as possible. We're all stunned. So soon? So far? Zena asks whether he can be accommodated in Albi, but the local children's home is full. Castres is a forty-minute drive away, but the director reassures her that Samer will still attend the same school as Anas: A bus service will get him there—he'll just need to get up a lot earlier in the mornings.

With heavy hearts, Zena, her parents, and I take Samer to Castres, and help him settle in over the course of the weekend. We're all very quiet on the way there, and that's a first since my Syrian family has been living with us. When we park outside the bright, spruce building, Samer is in tears. My stomach is in knots and I'm gripping the steering wheel fiercely. The director welcomes us, doing everything he can to put us at ease. He takes us to the studio where Samer will now be living: it's tiny but clean, functional, and fully furnished. It's in a building of about twenty similar studios, which is attached to the main building where the communal spaces are. The director explains that there's a central laundry where young residents must do their own washing. He tells us that an optional communal evening meal is offered, but all the studios have a kitchenette and residents are encouraged to prepare their own meals independently as soon as they can.

My throat feels constricted—Samer's just a boy! I remember when I was seventeen, what a privileged existence

I had with my mother doing everything for me. I think I'm right in saying I earned my first salary before making my first proper meal for myself.

It's time to leave and our goodbyes are heartbreaking, even though Samer does his best to be dignified, aware that he's being fast-tracked into adulthood with no time to prepare for it. Wafaa, who's sitting in the passenger seat on the way home, turns to me and whispers, "We'll cook for him on the weekends because he's going to lose more weight during the week."

The meeting in Toulouse is scheduled for the following Wednesday. Zena has tried her best to be prepared, collating every possible document and even the results of her father's medical tests. Over dinner on Tuesday evening, Saif Eddine is very gloomy.

"I don't know how it's going to go tomorrow, Stéphan, but I keep thinking about what happened in Hungary. Those brutes took our fingerprints by force, you know. That can't be a good sign."

Their meeting is at nine o'clock in the morning, and Zena has decided to take no chances so she leaves at 7:30. Neither of us has ever been to the prefectural office in Toulouse, which is in a magnificent early-eighteenth-century building, formerly the archbishop's palace. It's right in the city center, close to the cathedral, and parking is a challenge. Zena goes around in circles for twenty minutes before finding a space more than a kilometer away. When they finally arrive at the huge palace, the first hurdles are a walk-through metal detector and compulsory searches by the friendly security staff. Zena asks one of them where they need to go, and is directed to the third floor. At the top of the monumental staircase, a set of double doors leads to the relevant department. These doors open onto a waiting room whose chairs, as is invariably the case, are bolted to the floor, and a row of three counters—all of them closed with metal shutters. Opposite the doors, a long corridor leads off to the offices that handle applications for citizenship.

When Zena and her family arrive, all the seats in the waiting room are, of course, taken. There are already more than fifty people there. After chatting to some of them, Zena realizes that everyone is called for either 9 in the morning or 2 in the afternoon. It's not until nearly 9:30 that one of the metal shutters opens, and everyone immediately crowds around the counter. The woman at the desk makes an announcement, speaking up so that everyone can hear her:

"Ladies and gentlemen, we'll call you forward one family at a time to have your fingerprints taken."

She says this two or three times, then snaps the metal shutter closed again, and everyone sits back down slowly. Zena can see that her parents are panicking at the mention of fingerprints. They've heard—from people they met on their journey and from social media—about "dublinning" and asylum seekers being thrown out...A very large majority of the people around them are Syrian, and many of them are in the same situation and just as frightened. Zena has a long conversation with an elderly man, a Syrian who came to France forty years ago and is here to help his family by translating for them. Tall and very elegant with snow-white hair and a spectacular moustache, he reminds Zena of Damascus patriarchs and for a moment she loses herself in memories. He admits that he's very worried for his fellow countrymen: The situation in Syria is out of control, and European countries have all clamped down after making great promises about asylum...Who will offer them shelter? Who will save Syrian children?

Two young girls have given up their seats for Wafaa and Saif Eddine, who sit abjectly with their heads in their hands. The atmosphere across the whole waiting room is tense, stifling, faces are strained, bodies tired; babies cry and their mothers—blank faced, their minds on other things—take them out of their strollers to soothe them. One of the desks is open again and names are now called out at regular intervals in an apparently random order. It's a long wait. Staff members come through the waiting room to head off down the corridor toward the offices that handle applications for citizenship. Dressed in formal suits, some eye the refugees with near contempt, others simply ignore them. One or two do give them a "hello" when they first come through, but because they receive no reply, no acknowledgment, they soon give up this obviously superfluous courtesy.

The Al Khatib family is finally called just before eleven o'clock, and Zena and her relatives approach the desk. The olive-skinned woman at the window greets them with a smile and reiterates the fact that she will now take their fingerprints, although she doesn't explain why. She calls out each first name and pushes forward a small tablet on which they must press their fingers. She then slips out through the door behind her and disappears for a few minutes. She returns with this news:

"You've already requested asylum in another European country, Hungary, so it's up to Hungary to make a decision about your circumstances and to choose whether it would like to repatriate you—they have a two-month window in which to make this decision. I'm going to give each of you a document confirming that your case is pending, and you'll need to come back every two weeks to have it stamped to prove that you're still in France. Go back to the waiting room now, a social worker will come to see you in a few minutes."

Zena, my parents-in-law, Anas, and Mayada are devastated. Not very surprised, but horrified. Hungary? The country where they were subjected to the worst acts of cruelty, a place to which they have no ties of any kind, it makes no sense at all! Their lives and ambitions now

revolve around France, and nowhere else. How can anyone tell them they "requested asylum" in Hungary? They
asked for nothing at all, for goodness' sake, they just ended
up in a cell where their fingerprints were taken by force.
In France, an application for asylum is a detailed administrative file, a full account of the person's life, and an individual interview at the OFPRA.* In Hungary, is it just
having your fingerprints taken with threats of violence in
a filthy overcrowded cell? Where's the logic in all this?
Who writes these laws that only add to the misery of people who've already lost everything in their attempts to save
their own lives? Where's the humanity in it? Where's the
simple decency? Still, no one tries to argue or rail against
the woman who has delivered the news. They all accept
that there would be no point.

The thing we were dreading has happened: Saif, Wafaa,
Mayada, and Anas are now in the grips of the Dublin
Regulation, and will have to wait for Hungary to respond.
So two weeks later here they are back in Toulouse, going
through the soulless and meaningless procedure that they
will have to endure another three times.

An hour and fifteen minutes' drive, plus the time
spent parking.

---

* The French Office for the Protection of Refugees and Stateless Persons

Fifty people in the waiting room.

It's nine o'clock, the department's official opening time, but nothing's happening.

At ten o'clock, one desk opens and a voice asks everyone in the room to bring their "case pending" forms. The crowd gathers, forms are passed from hand to hand.

The desk closes again as soon as the last form has been taken.

Another hour's wait.

The comings and goings of employees handling citizenship applications continue. They study the ground and look away to avoid eye contact with the poor people who have come here for refuge.

The same solitary desk opens again and, in a monotonous drone, the voice calls families forward by name, one after the other.

When it is Zena's family's turn, the news is always the same: "Hungary hasn't replied. Here are your stamped forms. Come back in two weeks."

An hour and fifteen minutes' journey back to Albi.

And still the same uncertainty.

Which is increasingly difficult to take.

We do our best to support one another, savoring every moment we have together, but it's difficult. Even though Wafaa and Saif Eddine clearly enjoy being with us, they're always worried that they're in the way, a burden. As they see it, parents should look after their children and not be their dependents.

And then Wafaa hears about CADAs, shelters for asylum seekers.

"We can't go on invading your home like this," she says immediately. "We must apply for rooms in a CADA."

Zena's appalled.

"But Mom, Stéphan and I are happy you're here. And look at Julia, she adores you, you can't deprive her of your company."

But there's no changing Wafaa's mind, she won't give up. She only abandons the plan when Zena contacts the director of the CADA in Albi who tells her that none of the shelters for many kilometers around have any spaces.

Dr. R. still sees every member of the family regularly. More than once she advises all of them to see a psychiatrist at the hospital. She tells them about psychological trauma, the problems caused by their rootless existence, by losing everything when they left their country, the effects of the horrors they experienced on their journey, and the trials of adjusting to a culture so different from their own. But they all refuse, unanimous in this decision. It infuriates Zena because she has already consulted a psychologist and knows how useful therapy is. But she understands that this is cultural and all the arguments in the world won't make them change their minds. In Syria, seeing a psychiatrist or psychologist is viewed as a last resort for incurable mental cases and the feebleminded. Isabelle R. is right, though: They would all benefit from this sort of therapy, especially Anas. I'm discreetly keeping an eye on him and can see he's not gaining weight and still has the same dark rings under his eyes as when he arrived. His nights are constantly troubled by nightmares from which he wakes screaming. He can't be left alone in a room, even in broad daylight. We always leave a light on in the living room where he sleeps. The slightest sudden noise gives him terrible panic attacks. The poor boy's showing all the symptoms of post-traumatic stress disorder, and, if untreated, they'll dog him for years to come. Zena is endlessly attentive and thoughtful toward him. If he seems to like a meal, she and her mother keep making it until he won't touch it again. Saif drives him to school in the mornings, picks him up at the end of the day, and takes him along to do the grocery shopping.

"Tell me, Anas," I sometimes tease, "do you still have legs? Because you're being driven around so much they'll start to atrophy, don't you think?"

But Zena always flashes a furious look at me.

"He's tired, he needs all his strength for school."

I know exactly what she means. Let's mollycoddle him while we can. And anyway, I know that these outings are important to Saif, giving him something to do, making him feel useful. My father-in-law was such a busy man in Damascus, this is something he really needs.

Personally, I'm starting to struggle with being the tower of strength that I want to be for my family. I may be exhausted when I go to bed but I always toss and turn for hours before getting to sleep. I'm irritable and impatient at work even though I'm lucky to have a job I love. I've also altered my schedule a lot since Zena's family moved in with us, and none of my coworkers has commented. I've done this partly to spend more time with them, but also to support Zena who has so much on her plate: I arrive at the office a little later in the mornings and leave a lot earlier in the evenings. But there's no denying that my legendary optimism is gradually giving way to very unfamiliar defeatism. The glass half full— that used to be me. The one who stood tall when others were faltering—that used to be me. But my strength has its limits too and I no longer know how to be encouraging when Zena describes their trips to the prefectural office. I admit this only to myself in the secrecy of the night, but I'm starting to prepare myself for her family being deported, and I feel terribly guilty: If I'd planned my course of action better before going to Greece, they wouldn't have been forced to travel through the Balkan states and we wouldn't have come to this. Zena also tells me I might benefit from seeing a psychologist. She's worried because she can see that I'm growing more despondent by the day. But I refuse to, I grit my teeth and keep right on beating myself up, my self-criticism going around in circles—how could I be so naive and so powerless, both in Patras and here in France.

———

Just before Christmas the civil servant who hands Zena the stamped forms tells her that her family will not need to come back to Toulouse anymore.

"Hungary hasn't replied within the allotted time frame, so we can transfer your files to the prefectural office for the Tarn region in Albi. You need to go there in two weeks' time, I'll set up a meeting for you."

In the car on the way home, Zena and her family are all euphoric: Hungary hasn't made a move and that means they can stay in France! I don't say anything, I don't want to rain on their parade, but I certainly don't share their high spirits. In 2015, the prefecture in Tarn is reputed to be harsh in all its decision-making, and there are many stories on social media about its anti-immigrant stance: I'm still very worried about how this will all turn out.

In early January 2016 Zena and her family come home perplexed after their first meeting at the prefectural office in Albi.

"The people in Toulouse didn't send over our files yet, so we've been given another appointment."

Luckily, it wasn't a two-hour round trip this time.

In the meantime, Mayada has gone back to see Dr. R.: She still has terrible abdominal pains, has barely any appetite, and is losing more and more weight. She also recently started having inexplicable bouts of vomiting. The doctor decides to run a full set of diagnostic tests and the results are incontrovertible: Mimo has pancreatitis, a serious inflammation of the pancreas. By the time her diagnosis comes through, her life is in danger because at any moment she could be struck by necrosis of the pancreas, a hemorrhage, or septicemia. She is therefore given emergency surgery, but she will need five further operations before the doctors deem her to be out of danger. And there are side effects: For the rest of her life, Mayada will be dependent on heavy medication and will have to follow a draconian diet with no fats and no salt.

In mid-January Zena takes her family back to the prefectural office in Albi, and that's the day the sky falls in on them. Without a word of explanation, they are handed a letter addressed to Saif and his family, saying that the prefect for Tarn "plans to have them readmitted to Hungary"—in other words, deported, driven out of France—and giving them a week to make their case. A week! With no legal support or translation services offered. As soon as she is home with them, Zena calls me in tears. A week. How can anyone believe they're being given a proper chance to contest the decision to deport them? How do refugees cope if they have less support than Zena's family does? It's scandalous, a parody of correct procedure. I want to roar with anger, but I know it won't do any good. We must counterattack, and quickly. Zena specializes in penal law and I'm an expert in labor laws: Legal practitioners we may be, but we know nothing of European law. Never mind that, formulating a reply to fend off their deportation becomes an obsession from the moment we first see that letter, and we throw ourselves body and soul into the relevant texts to find our arguments. We focus frantically on one article in the Dublin III Regulation. The prefect is indeed in a position to deport dublinned asylum seekers because the regulation leaves this option open, even when the country in which they were dublinned has not come forward (and this is precisely the situation threatening Zena's family), but, according to article 17 of the same regulation, the prefect can also accept a request for asylum, even from people who have been dublinned. In a nutshell, Dublin III allows for a prefect to override Dublin III by deciding, without appeal, to consider applications for asylum from absolutely anyone in the world. But the prefect must want to do this . . . so we need to put forward some solid arguments.

We also look for a lawyer with expertise in this sort of case; it goes without saying that we don't know any ourselves, and we're soon disheartened when we type "lawyer specializing in refugees" into a search engine. Zena then thinks of turning to Terry Hugot, and it is Terry who puts us in touch with Mr. Brel in Toulouse. When Zena first gives me his name I do some research and find that he has already represented Syrian asylum seekers and has quite a high media profile—perfect. But from the very first phone call he tells us that he can make no direct contribution at this stage in the proceedings. All the same, he gives me some valuable advice to help us with our research, targeting specific articles in the Dublin III Regulation that have proved useful to him with other cases, and he tells me he would be prepared to contest the decision should it go against us.

Zena makes as much headway as she can during the day, and then after the evening meal she and I go through whatever information she has found that may help our case. But on the third evening, as soon as we're alone to work on the file she takes my hand.

"Stéphan," she says, "I did a test this morning. I'm pregnant."

I put down my pen, lost for words, and it takes me a moment to assimilate the news. Zena's pregnant! I'm overjoyed, throw my arms around her, and lift her off the floor, and she bursts out laughing.

"That's wonderful news, but...are you really sure?"

"Well, the result was clear enough, but I'll have a blood test next time we're at the clinic."

"It's a sign, don't you think? We must do everything we can to keep your parents here. This baby's come now to give us strength!"

"That's exactly what I thought, I was worried you'd think I've gone a little crazy..."

"Not at all, I mean, it's obvious. Are you feeling tired?"

"No, I'm fine! In fact, I found some interesting stuff about my father's health, I'll show you. I'll have to go see Dr. R., and I'm sure she'll agree to write a statement for us."

We go back to work, filled with new energy but still with pitifully few certainties. I'm devastated by Wafaa and Saif's optimism when they realize that Zena and I will be drafting their response. They know of their daughter's legal talents and have blind faith in me. We can't possibly let them down—we must succeed.

Zena and I eventually come up with a letter several pages long, signed by her father and supported by some fifty pages of documentation, including a statement from Dr. R. to confirm the diagnosis of my father-in-law's diabetes, a letter from the principal of Anas's school, a statement from the social worker about Zena's parents' finances, Zena's and Manal's birth certificates to prove their family relationships, our marriage certificate for the words "married to a Frenchman" . . . I send a copy of our letter and all the appended documents to Mr. Brel.

On the appointed day, Zena and I accompany Saif, Wafaa, Mimo, and Anas to the prefectural office where we have a meeting with the head of the Immigration and Integration Department. He has salt-and-pepper hair above a perfectly inexpressive face and a pair of fine-framed rectangular glasses. His tall, gray figure communicates only a chilly inflexibility. As he reaches toward the file that I've put before him on the desk, I preempt his gesture by opening it myself and launching into a detailed presentation of our letter and all the documents enclosed with it. His face tenses but he has no choice: He will listen to me, to the very end.

It goes without saying that the first "observation" we make in our reply is that my father-in-law had no intention of asking for asylum in Hungary and didn't even know that technically he had done so. He cannot contemplate returning to that country where he has no ties and where he and his family were beaten, brutalized, and arbitrarily incarcerated with no food or water. Hungary has in fact been the subject of European Commission investigations since December 2015 for procedural violations: Brussels is concerned that migrants whose right to asylum in Hungary is dismissed have great difficulty exercising their right to appeal or being heard by an impartial court.

Our letter also highlights Saif's state of health. His serious diabetes means he needs daily doses of insulin, and, financially, he is entirely dependent on Zena and me. One of the articles in the Dublin III Regulation anticipates precisely this sort of case:

> *Where, on account of pregnancy, a newborn child, serious illness, severe disability or old age, an applicant is dependent on the assistance of his or her child, sibling or parent legally resident in one of the Member States, or his or her child, sibling or parent legally resident in one of the Member States is dependent on the assistance of the applicant, Member States shall normally keep or bring together the applicant with that child, sibling or parent, provided that family ties existed in the country of origin, that the child, sibling or parent or the applicant is able to take care of the*

dependent person and that the persons concerned
expressed their desire in writing.

Zena is married to a Frenchman, has the appropriate residence permit, and her sister Manal was granted political
refugee status by OFPRA in February 2015. The director's face remains perfectly impassive during my whole
presentation, and it's abundantly clear that there would
be no point in asking for his opinion or any indication of
the possible outcome. He simply brings the meeting to an
end with a bland, "We'll study your file and get back to
you very soon."

To my great surprise he calls me the same afternoon.

"Is your father-in-law's diabetes type I or type II? The
doctor's letter doesn't specify."

Zena races off to the clinic to discuss this with Dr. R.

"Your father actually has type II diabetes," the doctor says, frowning. "Nonspecialists sometimes consider
it benign in comparison with type I because of mistaken
assumptions like, for example, type II diabetics aren't
insulin-dependent. Don't worry, I'll write you a solid
statement."

Zena leaves with a letter stating that "Mr. Al Khatib
suffers from severe diabetes equivalent to type I, and
needs daily insulin treatments." I scan the letter so that
it's ready for the director the next morning.

A few days after our meeting, Saif receives a letter
summoning him to the prefectural office on February 11.

I can't join them, but it's the department director himself who sees Zena and her family again.

With a subtle smile playing on his lips, he tells Saif, "The prefect has reached his decision and I will give you a copy in writing. You are to be deported with your wife and two children."

At this point Zena tries to interject but he raises an imperious hand and continues, still smiling, "Unfortunately, I can't provide you with plane tickets immediately today but, believe me, it will be quick. In the meantime, you and the three other family members affected by this ruling will be under house arrest."

Zena calls me moments later and tells me she couldn't hold back her emotions: She burst into tears at the sheer cruelty of this man who clearly took pleasure in telling a whole family he was sending them to hell. I can hear all the others crying behind her. I, meanwhile, am savagely angry.

A few hours later I read the letter that the director handed to my father-in-law. Yes, these are the facts: The prefect of the Tarn region makes no allowances for the factors we set out for him and has drafted a prefectural decree in which he "entrusts Mr. Al Khatib to the Hungarian authorities who are responsible for considering his application for asylum." And, therefore, to deport the whole family to Hungary. Even worse, the decision is coupled with house arrest, as if they were common terrorists, and the family must "clock in" at the police precinct twice a week.

Two people nearing their sixties and in fragile health, a high school boy, and a very sick young woman between two vital surgeries: That's the gang of terrible criminals posing such a threat to French national security that each and every one of them needs to be under house arrest. It makes me so angry and ashamed, ashamed of my country, ashamed of individuals who claim to serve the state by turning away desperate people whose only ambition is to survive. What on earth does this prefect think the Al Khatibs are doing here? Sightseeing? Does he really believe they've chosen France after "benchmarking" social aid across Europe, to use the words of I-don't-remember-which politician whom I don't want to pay the respect of naming? I wish I could send all these heartless monsters to Syria for a month so they could understand. Understand that no human being would put him or herself through a journey as harrowing as the one my parents-in-law undertook out of notional "greed." What would they possibly stand to gain? All the Syrians I know had flourishing careers in their own country: engineers, doctors, specialized craftsmen, lawyers . . . they had a comfortable standard of living, owned at least one house, had cars and paid for their children's private educations. And it's because they had the means that they could finance their journey to France. By leaving Syria they lost everything, and they did it to save the single most important thing: their own skins. Here, to their total despair, they're mostly out of work. They're haunted by the shame of having to live off benefits, and they fight to avoid being reduced to this. But very few of them succeed in having their professional qualifications recognized, and if they do, their years of experience in Syria are never taken into account.

So now my father-in-law is under house arrest with his box of insulin. But it gets worse. This absurd ruling automatically reduces the time that Zena's family has to challenge the new decision . . . to just two days. Forty-eight hours to decide the lives of an entire family. But we planned ahead and have been in touch with the relevant lawyer for nearly a month: the tall, athletic thirtysomething Mr. Brel agrees to see us right away.

He confirms that the file Zena and I put together is perfectly on track, and decides to take on the administrative tribunal. He continues to rely on our arguments but also puts before the tribunal official reports of how badly asylum seekers are treated in Hungary, alongside the fact that Zena's other sister, Mirvat, who stayed in Syria, has just obtained a visa for France with a view to asking for asylum. In a ruling made on February 16, the court revokes the decision to deport the family and instructs the Tarn prefect to reexamine the file.

The threat has been avoided, but the administrative tribunal has set no time limit on the Tarn prefect. Weeks and months go by, Zena's stomach grows bigger, but her family's applications make no headway. We haven't heard a word from the Tarn prefecture since the ruling from the administrative tribunal. To be blunt, they've ground to a halt.

My mother-in-law grows restless and starts fretting about how guilty she feels again.

"We've invaded your house for so long now," she tells Zena, "it's not right!"

My father-in-law is bored, he can't bear having no purpose and nothing to do, he feels useless. I sometimes catch him standing at a window with his hands behind his back, his eyes blank. He lost everything when he left Syria, and he can't find where he really belongs in France. Does he regret coming? Meanwhile, Mayada shuts herself in her bedroom, coming out only if Julia calls her, and spends hours on the phone with friends who stayed in Damascus. She too gave up part of her life, and it's hard, particularly with her health problems.

My parents-in-law often call their daughter in Orléans, and Manal talks more and more about them going back to live with her. She has done some research and is convinced that the prefecture in the Loiret region looks far more favorably on refugees, so they would be granted asylum and even given housing. If they moved and had their file transferred, it could be a real opportunity for them: Every prefecture has its own policies for applying the directives and legislation concerning refugees.

Saif broaches the subject for the first time over dinner one evening, but Zena refuses even to listen.

"We're a long way through the process with the pre-fecture in Albi, I'm sure it'll get through. And there's plenty of space for you here, you know it would be very different at Manal's place."

This is hard for Zena; I know she's always dreamed of having her family here, near her. But Saif raises the sub-ject again in private with me a few days later, and I can understand his distress—this absurd waiting game has dragged on for nearly nine months now. I try my best to talk to my wife and the topic crops up repeatedly in other conversations . . . and Zena gradually comes to understand that she can't keep them here by force. We sit down and discuss the idea again, and reach an agreement: We must let them go.

12

New lives

We're shell-shocked when the four of them leave in May, but we're also happy and relieved for their sakes: There was no future for them in Tarn... perhaps there is in Loiret. And they also need to be more autonomous in their day-to-day lives. So long as they were here they all relied too heavily on Zena who, truth be told, wanted to be there for them every minute of the day. So she would drive Anas all over the place, convinced he wouldn't manage otherwise. When he arrives at Manal's house he immediately demonstrates that he's perfectly capable of catching a bus to go wherever he wants.

Manal was right, and everything changes for my parents-in-law and their children one day in June 2016 when the clerk manning the only open desk at the prefecture in

Orléans hands them a receipt to acknowledge their application for asylum. This simple piece of paper is a huge victory: It confirms that it will indeed be France, and not Hungary, that handles their application. It is valid for only a month but can be renewed until they are given a definitive reply to their request for asylum. On the other hand, they have only twenty-one days to put together their official application for asylum with OFPRA, enclosing a full account of their lives, in French, and explaining why they would not be safe to return home to Syria. When OFPRA has had time to digest their application, they are given appointments in the Paris region—the organization has no other premises. Each member of the family must be interviewed individually, with the help of an interpreter, to go back over his or her personal story and describe his or her current circumstances. They are told there and then that they can expect to wait between three and six months for an answer.

However long the waiting time, this receipt means that Saif, Wafaa, and their children are now officially asylum seekers, with all the associated rights. As soon as they have this document in their hands, my parents-in-law tell Manal and Khaled they're leaving: The apartment is too small for ten of them to live together comfortably and they can't bear this constant feeling that they're invading and in the way. Despite Manal and Khaled's protestations, my parents-in-law stand their ground. Manal backs down and starts using the network of contacts she has built up through her translating work for the OFII* to find them accommodation in a CADA, starting in July. My mother-in-law calls Zena in a state of excitement—she will have a home of her own at last!

But the day they move into the apartment that they have been allocated in Joué-lès-Tours comes as a cold shower. They are to share the space with a family from Chechnya. They don't know each other and don't even have a common language. Each family has two private bedrooms and its own toilets, but all the other spaces are shared: living room, kitchen, and bathroom. Zena feels for her poor mother, who felt awkward sharing a house with her own family...she must be going through hell with these strangers, however courteous and respectful they are. And even though Wafaa tries to put a brave face on it, Anas eventually admits to Zena that their sheer timidity means they daren't sit in the living room if the other family is in there, so they spend their evenings in their bedrooms. All the same, as the months go by, it becomes clear that everyone in the household wants this cohabiting to work as well as possible and the two families pull together— although Wafaa will never come to terms with even cooking at the same time as the other mother. Still, there is one very positive aspect to this CADA: the support that refugees are given in everything they do. Whether they have an appointment with the doctor, the welfare office, the

---

* The French Agency for Immigration and Integration

unemployment office, or the prefecture, Saif and Wafaa are never left to fight it out on their own, and this gives them true peace of mind—as it does us because, at such a distance, we can't give them this support ourselves.

Two wonderful pieces of news finally brighten 2016, which has been a very dark year.

In September 2016 Zena gives birth to a girl who's perfect in every way. Our little Mila. Julia is as thrilled as we are, she adores her baby sister and brings her soft toys whenever she hears her cry. The house felt very empty after Wafaa, Saif, Mayada, and Anas left but it's filled to the brim with love again now!

Then, in October, my parents-in-law receive confirmation that France is granting them political refugee status, and the longest period of protection available—ten years—because OFPRA recognizes the life-threatening danger they would face in their own country. We're delighted with this news, and Zena now knows for sure that she was right to let them leave. They can start building their own lives here at last. Knowing that the French authorities acknowledge their suffering, understand that they had no choice but to flee, and guarantee their safety by offering them a permanent home is genuinely a rebirth for them.

13.

Happiness with no clouds on the horizon

ZENA'S STORY

September 2017.

A beautiful summer is coming to an end.

My parents are offered social housing and can move out of the CADA where they've been living since leaving Manal's home. I'm so glad to see them properly settled. They were granted political refugee status a little under a year ago and now have a guarantee that they can stay in France, in safety. We hear regularly from Samer, who's flourishing in France, despite the heartbreak of failing to get his mother to come join him.

It feels like we can breathe at last. Julia is four and Mila just turned one. Our family life is the same as millions of other families in France: happy and chaotic! I haven't returned to work since Mila was born because I've had various health problems, but I'm still making progress with my thesis: I've written nearly two hundred pages and plan to finish before June 2018. I also do various translating jobs.

The Greek episode is now nothing more than a distant memory for us all. Toward the end of the summer of 2015, Stéphan wrote to the French consulate in Athens, asking them to recommend a bilingual lawyer. We were pointed in the direction of Mrs. D., a lawyer and honorary consul. Stéphan called her to explain his case and since then she has kept an eye on the timetable of legal proceedings and said she would warn us if anything happened. We have not heard from her since.

Every now and then, perhaps over a meal at a family gathering, someone will ask Stéphan, "What about the car, where did you get with that?"

"Nowhere, we don't really have much information."

"But are you trying to find out more?"

"Yes, but we've had no news from the lawyer, and every person or organization that we contact toys with us for a while and then says they need payment before they can supply us with a document or have something translated . . . We don't have the budget for it! And anyway, we keep thinking that when they decide they want to contact us, they'll go right ahead."

14.

When your world
falls apart and the
sky falls in

Wednesday, September 20, 2017. I'm just coming out of a meeting that dragged on all morning. The beginnings of a migraine are quietly threatening and I head for the coffee machine to eradicate them. While my cup fills, I scroll through my personal emails on my cell phone. In among the usual messages there's something unexpected: Mrs. D. is getting in touch at last. I haven't heard from her for nearly two years.

From: Christina D.
Sent: Wednesday September 20, 2017 11:46
To: Stéphan Pélissier
Subject: Trial 11.9.2017

Dear Mr. Pélissier,

Your trial has been set for November 9 2017 please let
me know if you want to defend yourself

Sincerely Christina D. Attorney at Law French Honorary
Consul

I immediately email her asking for more information
and she tells me nothing but arranges for us to have a
telephone conversation that same evening, at 6:30 PM
French time.

When I call Zena at lunchtime to see how she's doing,
I mention the email. We're both kind of pleased, and neither of us has the tiniest inkling that this could get complicated. We just think we'll finally have our car back, and
our only concern is how much it might cost. Given that it
all happened in Greece in the first place, we think there's
bound to be a fine or some kind of duty, something to
grease the wheels...

"If they're too greedy, we'll just leave it there!" I tell
Zena, laughing. "I mean, we've coped without it for two
years, haven't we?"

Zena gives the girls their bath every night at 6:30, but
we both feel she should be with me on the call with the
lawyer, so, just for today, Julia's watching a cartoon and
Mila's playing in her playpen. After the usual greetings, I
feel like I've had a sack of cement dumped on me, because
Mrs. D. tells me this has nothing to do with my car.

She breaks the news that this is actually about me, I'm being sued.

I close my eyes for a moment. I don't understand any of this. The things she's saying make no sense.

I ask her to explain, but all she does is reiterate that the Greek Ministry of Justice is pursuing a case against me and my trial will be in early November, as she wrote in her email. In order for her to have access to the case file and—crucially—the reasons for this suit, I must first officially appoint her as my lawyer and pay an up-front fee of five hundred euros. On autopilot, I ask her to email me, confirming what I need to do. Before hanging up she tells me she'll be able to give me more information within forty-eight hours: She will ask to have access to the prosecutor's report as soon as I return the documents appointing her as my legal adviser on the case.

I put down the phone, shaking my head in disbelief. Zena's eyes are full of questions, she can tell something bad is happening. I tell her what I know, in other words, if I'm honest, not very much, but her eyes widen in horror: The word "trial" is enough to haul us both back to that dark chapter of our lives that we thought was closed. I hurriedly fill out the forms that the lawyer sent me—we need to be done with this frightening suspense as soon as possible.

Mrs. D. calls back two days later; Zena and I haven't really slept or eaten since her first call. She details the charges against me: I'm being prosecuted for the mass illegal transportation of persons with no official documents. Put bluntly, as far as the Greek justice system is concerned, I'm a people smuggler. The only consolation is that I don't need to attend the trial myself, my lawyer can represent me.

I'm reeling from the shock. This feels like a terrible nightmare but with the anguish of being perfectly awake and conscious, knowing it's real and could dramatically change my life, our lives. The lawyer ends the conversation by telling me that, if found guilty, I would be liable for nine years' imprisonment. I'm appalled and overwhelmed but I also chafe rebelliously: The family relationships that I proved in 2015 by showing my family records book to the examining magistrate don't feature in the prosecutor's report, only in my statement.

I suddenly feel very small, caught up in a huge soulless machine that's going to crush me. The fact that the family records book isn't mentioned is catastrophic. Was this a deliberate omission? Is my case being used as an example to Europeans who want to go and help refugees, to all the people whose "solidarity" is criticized by the justice system that deems them guilty of an offense? The examining magistrate studied that family records book right in front of me, she said nothing that led me to believe she wouldn't document it. I was taken for a ride. I'm trapped between arbitrary procedures and judicial errors . . . and I can't see a way out.

In the days after the lawyer's call, Zena and I are battered against the rocky walls of anxiety and insomnia.

Devastated by news of the trial and aware of how much time and energy she will devote to preparing my defense, Zena very reluctantly decides she must abandon her thesis. I, meanwhile, keep my teeth clenched all day, unable to concentrate on anything, physically at work but mentally absent, on autopilot with my daughters and, although I may fall asleep easily, it is only to wake up drenched in sweat at 3 AM, incapable of going back to sleep.

These lines from Baudelaire's poem "Condemned Women" echo inside my head: "I feel such heavy dread dissolving over me [...] Beneath a bloody sky that closes all around."

15.

Dear Mr. Pélissier, the French president has asked me . . .

s soon as I hung up with Mrs. D., I emailed the French consulate in Athens to inform them of the situation. Their reply comes back swiftly on Monday: Greece is a sovereign country and it is not possible to intervene in matters handled by an independent justice system . . . to be honest, I was expecting this. Over Sunday lunch I was already telling my parents, "I'm going to write to the president himself!" Sandra was dubious and my father thought it over the top. But my mind was made up, and still is. And anyway, this means I can do something, and that's what I need if I'm to stay sane. It wouldn't be accurate to say calm is restored, but the moment I start contacting politicians about my case, I find it a little easier to sleep.

Time being of the essence, I go straight to the website for the Élysée Palace. No email address is listed, but I find a "Contact Us" form in which I give a quick outline of my situation and ask for help from the presidency. But I need to give fuller, more precise details, and over the course of the next week I draft and send a three-page letter to the French president, Emmanuel Macron. In it I describe the nightmare experienced by my in-laws before they left Syria, as well as my ordeal being held in custody in Greece and supplying my family record book to the court. I describe my astonishment when, nearly two years after the incident, I found that I am to be tried as a people smuggler. "I am therefore being prosecuted for trying to save my father-in-law, mother-in-law, brother-in-law, and sister-in-law. Prosecuted like a common criminal, by a European state." Before ending the letter with a request to the president for diplomatic intervention to restore justice and humanity, I cite the articles of French law that reassured me, just before I left, about the legality of my undertaking:

> Article L. 622-4 of the Code of Entry and Stay of
>   Aliens and Right of Asylum (CESEDA)...
>   assisting an irregular nonnational to stay
>   illegally in France will not give rise to criminal
>   prosecution on the basis of Articles L. 622-
>   1...when the assistance is provided by

1) ascendants or descendants of the nonnational
    or his/her spouse, brothers or sisters of the
    nonnational or his/her spouse;

2) the spouse of the nonnational, or a person who
    cohabits with the nonnational, or the parents,
    children, brothers, or sisters of the spouse of the
    nonnational or of the person who cohabits with
    the nonnational;

3) any person who provides legal advice or the
    provision of food, accommodation, or medical
    care to ensure dignified and decent living
    conditions for the nonnational, or any other
    assistance to preserve the dignity or the health
    and well-being of the nonnational, providing
    that this assistance does not give rise to any
    direct or indirect compensation.

On September 29 I have a surprise: an email from
the Élysée Palace. The presidency has replied, and so
promptly! I can already picture people leaping to my aid,
but my happiness dissolves as soon as I understand the
content of the email, which is signed by the president's
principal private secretary. I'm informed, in essence,
that the principle of Greek sovereignty doesn't allow the
French president to intervene. Nevertheless, I'm told that
my correspondence has been passed on to Mrs. Nathalie
Louiseau, minister for European affairs.

In the time between that first email from my lawyer and the date of my trial, I also contact the prime minister's office, but they don't demonstrate the same responsiveness: It takes more than a month for them to reply with a simple email telling me that my request will be passed on to the attorney general, Nicole Belloubet, and the secretary of state, Jean-Yves Le Drian.

In the meantime, we've heard that my trial has been deferred. Zena collapses when I read her the email from Mrs. D. informing us of the delay, and I understand her distress: We can't take any more, this needs to end, one way or another. I want to know my fate, I want to know what's going to happen to my life.

In the end the trial takes place on November 29, and, despite my efforts to inform the French authorities, my lawyer really will be the only person defending my case. I'm forced to acknowledge—bitterly—that my country is not behind me.

Even though, at least in the first instance, this reaps no better rewards, I also contact several local elected representatives, including the senator for the Tarn, Philippe Bonnecarrère. This former mayor of Albi is now vice president of the Committee for European Affairs at the Senate, a sincere and committed man who is the first politician to offer me any assistance, and whose support never slackens.

Principal private Secretary
to the President of the Republic
Monsieur Stéphan PÉLISSIER
[Address obscured]

Paris, September 28, 2017

Dear Mr. Pélissier,

The President of the Republic has asked me to reply to the correspondence you addressed to him.

I would have willingly offered you assistance but the principle of individual state sovereignty does not allow the presidency of the French Republic to intervene in the case to which you refer.

I have nevertheless forwarded your correspondence to the minister responsible for European affairs, who works alongside the minister for Europe and foreign affairs, in order that she be aware of your case.

Yours sincerely,

François-Xavier LAUCH
Reference for all correspondence
[text redacted]

16.

Raising awareness
and media coverage

'm very pessimistic about the trial and its outcome, but I can't let myself be beaten down. No, I want to fight with all my might. And these first exchanges with the world of politics quickly prove that appealing single-handedly to the authorities for support in an extraterritorial case is virtually pointless. This therefore validates a choice that I made at a very early stage, before even receiving the verdict from the court in Patras: We must warn the public, we must let the French people know the fate meted out to one of their kind who simply wanted to save his family, so I decide to secure as much media coverage as possible.

I already have a small network of contacts. When Zena's parents arrived in September 2015, I naturally told my coworkers about their struggle. One of them had a son on an internship at the regional newspaper *La Dépêche du Midi*; one thing led to another and a very positive, feel-good sort of article appeared under the headline "Refugees Reunited with Their Tarn family." The article attracted the attention of other local media, spawning an article in *Le Tarn libre*, an interview on local radio, and even a piece on France 3 regional TV.

I've kept in touch with these contacts, as I have with Ghislaine Buffard, the director who was interested in Manal and Khaled's story. I informed them all when my parents-in-law looked likely to be deported to Hungary, and let them know about the case that Mr. Brel brought against the Tarn prefect. Ghislaine and quite a crowd of journalists were at the administrative court on the day of the trial.

Which is why, as soon as Mrs. D. uses the words "crime" and "people smuggler," I know I must resort to this form of leverage. It's obvious, an absolute necessity, offering a tiny glimmer of hope to help me get out of the situation in which I find myself.

"We have no chance at all if we just sit doing nothing with no one helping us," I tell Zena. "We have nothing to lose, it's bound to help!"

And so, two years after the administrative hearing in Toulouse, I get back in touch with my contacts in radio, television, and the press. Éric Berger at *La Dépêche* is one of the first to react: He is someone I will always think of as a friend, and he does a lot to ensure our story is made public, not only in his newspaper but also among his own network of journalists in other media. The second pillar of our media coverage is Christophe Chassaigne at France 3 Tarn: He follows our case right from the start, with true dedication and genuine goodwill. The other media—be they press, radio, or TV—will only ever give us coverage at the instigation of Éric or Christophe.

In the first instance, only print media approaches me. I'm reasonably comfortable in this medium. I'm used to writing for my work, putting together documents with strong ideas supported by explanatory appendices; plus it can be done "cold," at a distance. La Dépêche soon asks me to appear in a short video that they can use on their website, and this also poses few problems: They're happy to cut and start again if I ask them to, and the interviewer asks me what I want to talk about, to be sure that he puts the relevant questions to me.

Things get trickier when it comes to doing radio and TV interviews. I'm used to public speaking: I'm a social relations legal expert, I contribute to important meetings on a near daily basis and have to put my point across in front of fifteen or twenty people. But being interviewed is totally different! I like to think of the media as a platform, but the truth is I have no guarantee that the three or four important ideas that I desperately want to get across can be shoehorned into my replies to whatever questions the interviewer asks, questions I never know ahead of time. I'm keen to communicate the fact that my in-laws' lives were at risk both in Syria and while they were fleeing; that France doesn't prosecute people who help family members to escape; and that Zena and I lead a simple, ordinary life with our daughters. So I need to stay completely calm, or at least appear so, because the camera (or the mic) takes no prisoners, but I must also give as good as I get from the journalist, without losing track of where he or she is heading.

Anyone would be stressed at the thought of being interviewed live, on a subject close to his or her heart, while in a dangerous situation like mine. But that's not all: While I prepare frantically for each of these interviews, I'm hiding a secret weakness . . . all through my childhood and up until I was at university I had a stutter. All those years spent terrified that the words wouldn't come out of my mouth and furious that I knew what I wanted to say but couldn't say it—they now came back to haunt me when I thought I'd put them behind me long ago. I had no therapy at the time and no specific form of support. I coped on my own, doing my own research and working on the problem independently. My tenacity was supported by love from my family and my faith in God, which is as far-reaching as it is independent of any religion. It's funny because, like most people who've had a stutter, I'm very talkative and I've chosen a career where oral expression is crucial: I have to speak in presentations, to negotiate, to persuade other people and sometimes even to confront them. I'm perfectly at ease in the moment, but when I'm anticipating a particularly difficult meeting, I have an irrational fear that my stutter will come back like the shark in *Jaws* suddenly looming out of the water and violently overturning the boat on which I'm trying to escape.

When I start doing TV interviews, there's the same ambivalence between the relaxed Stéphan and the Stéphan who once had a stutter. I'll never forget my first live TV experience on the news show *19/20* for France 3 Tarn on September 29. When we arrive at the France 3 premises in Toulouse, we're shown around the studios and the newsroom to put us at ease. Despite this warm welcome, I'm very aware that I'll be talking live, with no safety net: I'm ashen-faced, almost paralyzed with fear, and poor Zena runs out of ways to reassure me. I've brought a few notes so that I have something to cling to like a buoy. Just before we start filming, the interviewer takes me aside. I think he's going to tell me what his questions will be, but he just gives me an idea of what he'll be discussing with me. When he sees the sheets of paper in my hands, he gives me some advice.

"If you don't mind my saying," he says, "don't use notes and, whatever happens, don't try to get across some message you've prepared. I've already seen people mess up interviews trying to do that. We have just five minutes: If you give long answers in order to make a point, I'll only have time for a couple of questions and you won't get through to people in the same way."

He's right to warn me, I would have fallen straight into that trap. I stow my notes back in my briefcase and decide to put my faith in my instincts and this man's genuine intention to help me tell my story. And I do have a little experience: I've been doing press and radio interviews for a few days now so I have a clear idea of what I want to say.

It's my turn to speak, I'm replying to the first question: "They're running away from mortal danger, they're victims, they're family, I go to help them and now I'm told that we're the criminals."

On screen I look drawn, worn down by events but also profoundly outraged and this anger sustains me, helps me stand tall and strong at such a difficult time.

Those words were improvised, they came to me spontaneously. When interviews are shorter, like the one for CNews which lasts just two minutes, I start to understand—though not necessarily to forgive—politicians who trot out for every interview the same short, high-impact sentence prepared with their staff. I don't have the luxury of a speechwriter, but I'm fully aware that, with so little available time, you have to hammer out a few key statements to grab attention, ensure you're understood, and hope viewers will still remember you tomorrow.

In the early days I emerge from these interviews totally frazzled, exhausted by the huge effort I've put into answering questions while frantically thinking of a way to communicate—in just a few words—the things I want to say, without turning into a robot or seeming insincere.

"There were sixty-five of them on an eight-meter boat."

"They nearly drowned."

"I haven't stolen anything or killed anyone."

"I'm not a hero or a criminal."

One of the assistants at Mila's day nursery is especially attentive. She always has a kind word and a smile, and when Zena told her I might be facing a prison sentence because I helped her parents, she was very affected by the news. She regularly asks for updates and shows Mila the affection that my little girl so badly needs in all this turmoil. One evening in late October I happen to be the one picking Mila up from the day nursery. As I'm leaving, the assistant asks me if I've thought of mounting a petition.

"You know, on Facebook," she says. "Everyone does it, why shouldn't you? What's happening to you is really serious."

I discuss it with Zena when I get home, and she agrees that it's an excellent idea. And so we set up our petition addressed to Emmanuel Macron on Change.org.

17.

An unbearable
waiting game

The days are punctuated by letters and interviews, and we're growing increasingly pessimistic: We think I'll be sentenced to one year in prison, perhaps as a suspended sentence, perhaps not. Zena and I both have substantial doubts about my lawyer's competence. Since my last telephone conversation with her in late September, despite my requests, she hasn't sent me any French translations of legal documents that might shed more light on my situation. And she's never free to talk to me. At this distance I have no traction with her, and I feel happier concentrating on my aim of bringing our story to the attention of the French public and letting it build momentum. My lawyer finally contacts us a few days before the trial to say she's found a verdict for a similar case in

Patras: The defendant was discharged. She reads through the court's decision, which is of course written in Greek, and doesn't translate it even though I chose her because she speaks French. I will later learn that the Greek press got wind of my story and several local journalists asked to interview her but she systematically refused.

Every day that my lawyer does nothing toward my case adds to my wife's despair.

"She's our only contact, our only hope, and she's not doing anything! I'm a lawyer too, Stéphan, and I've never treated a client like this."

All the same, Zena does everything she can to reassure her parents, dreading the thought that they will blame themselves. At this stage, Saif and Wafaa are confident about the outcome.

"There won't be a sentence," they tell Zena. "We told them straightaway that we're his wife's parents, we made it very clear he's not a dealer but a member of the family. There won't be a sentence and do you know what? You'll get your car back."

I'm also worried about my own parents and sister; I know that they're finding this very stressful, although they try not to let it show. The whole family is on tenter-hooks, and I can't think of any way to reassure them about this terrible, precarious case in the hands of a lawyer with such a casual attitude.

18.

Seven years in prison

ZENA'S STORY

When Stéphan finally gets a hold of his lawyer, I watch him screw up his face as he listens to the verdict. *My God*, I think immediately, *he's got a year in prison*. He hangs up and sits in silence for a moment. When he eventually manages to repeat the words that have so visibly shaken him, I myself am poleaxed:

"Seven years. I've been sentenced to seven years in prison with no possibility of parole."

I don't know what to say. Stéphan looks away, briefly gazes at the kitchen table where we're sitting, and picks up an imaginary crumb. Then he rubs his forehead, rubs all over his head as if trying to force himself back into the room.

"And the sentence is redeemable."

"What does 'redeemable' mean?"

"It's very simple: five euros per day of the sentence, so a total of thirteen thousand euros."

I can't believe it, this is like being back in Syria. A redeemable sentence? You can buy your freedom in a European country that's meant to be a democracy? If you ask me, this is a corrupt system in broad daylight, for all to see. It's almost worse than the prison sentence: It just adds to our total lack of understanding, and our disgust. In a few hours' time, it will give us hope, but right now it just makes us sick.

"Of course the lawyer's advising me to appeal."

"Do you think that's a good idea?"

"No, wait, I can't accept this verdict! What does it say? That I'm a common criminal, a people smuggler, a mercenary who makes money off of other people's misery? I want to clear my name. We've got grounds, Zena, moral and legal grounds—this case isn't over."

"But think about it: What's the point? I can't see how the court could reduce its sentence from seven years with no parole to a discharge or even an acquittal..."

"I'm sure they could, rulings get overturned like that all over the world. At least if you can give the court a good reason, and I can give them plenty!"

"If Greece were still an honest country, maybe, but—I mean really!—a redeemable prison sentence? That tells the whole story. You're bound to lose."

Should he appeal? Another year, possibly two, of sleepless nights and anxious days? No. No! I can't take it, I just wouldn't get through it. All the guilt that I managed to sweep under the rug in our peaceful family life, the feeling that I was responsible for sending my husband off to be arrested and therefore sentenced to prison...all that now comes crashing down on me with shocking violence.

It seems obvious to me: It would be better to pay. Yes, but how? Those thirteen thousand euros are funds we just don't have.

19.

Guilty of loving

First the news of the trial and then this unconsciona-ble verdict—our whole family suffers the blow of our brush with the Greek legal system.

When my father first heard about the trial he took it very badly, echoing the way he reacted when I set off to Greece without warning him. He criticized me for precisely the faults I see in myself, told me how naive I'd been, kept saying I walked right into the lion's den. Our conversations resonated painfully with my own feelings of guilt, a fiercely corrosive emotion that ate away at me day and night. If only I'd been smarter, if only I'd prepared a proper plan of action to get us all onto that ferry. I relived our arrest one second at a time every night, and

thought through all the other options we could have chosen to succeed.

Although my mother hadn't spoken to me about this,
I'm sure she's told my father how deeply his criticism
affected me. Thanks to her and because, first and fore-
most, he wanted to support me like the good head of
the household that he is, he calmed down and demonstrated that he was right behind me, whatever the cost.
And so did my sister. United around me, my family was
a valuable support when that unacceptable verdict was
delivered.

I try my best to hold it together after the verdict. I have a
wonderful wife and two gorgeous little girls, my coworkers
are supportive, and I can see that our attempts to raise the
profile of our case are starting to produce results...But,
oh my goodness, it's hard to keep going. Seven years in
prison! We hear on the news every day about murderers
and rapists who are given shorter sentences. Despite my
best efforts, I'm gloomy, often dejected, not always there
for my children or my wife, even though she really needs
me. Our younger daughter, Mila, can feel the change and
she lets it show. She slept through the night very early but
now can't sleep alone and cries for hours every evening despite all our efforts to soothe her. Julia is bearing up well,
although she's amazed to see her daddy on TV. Zena and I

try to tell her what's going on and her teacher tells us later that Julia explained it all to her.

"Daddy's a hero," Julia told her. "He saved Granny and Grandpa when they died in the sea!"

The time that the four of us spend together is precious to me, radiant. When we're with our daughters we feel good, we're in the moment, and everything else disappears for a while. But even these wonderful times can't heal the wounds that my time in custody in Greece, and now this trial, have opened in me. I'm irritable and I fly off the handle with Zena and the girls. I immediately regret it but there's so much anger in me that it's often more than I can contain.

When we're given the verdict, Saif and Wafaa are horrified and can't forgive themselves for the problems they feel they brought on me. My mother-in-law, despite being very reserved, takes the trouble to call me straightaway to apologize.

"It's all our fault, Stéphan, we're so sorry."

I do what I can to convince her that the responsibility lies not with her or me but the outrageous and inhuman workings of the Greek justice system. It makes me furious to hear this woman—whom I love like a second mother—crying over the situation. Only my sisters-in-law prove relatively serene, and I'm glad that they are: It means that Zena can rely on their warmth and support, and she needs that. Manal in particular puts her faith in rallying public opinion. She remembers the positive effect that Ghislaine Buffard's report had on her family's life.

We have a limited window of time. We must decide whether or not to appeal, and we have only ten days to make this decision. When the lawyer told me that I'd been sentenced to prison with no remission, my instinct was to refute the verdict. But everyone close to us—both friends and relations—has the same reaction...

"Thirteen thousand euros?" they say. "Well, we'll all chip in and help you. Don't get embroiled in another trial."

And so Zena persuades me to go down this route.

"We'll see, Stéphan, but I do think we should try to set up a kitty. Let's see how much we have just before the deadline and then make a decision."

Our families are obviously our first donors and we're deeply touched by their generosity. It isn't enough, though; far from it. But everything changes thanks to a phone call I receive the day after the verdict.

"Hello, Mr. Pélissier, this is Vincent Lesclauze at Bangumi Productions."

Neither of these names means anything to me.

"Hello...erm, do we know each other?"

"Not yet. I work with Yann Barthès on the TV show *Quotidien*. Yann has heard about your story and we'd like to have you and your wife on the show."

Yann Barthès! *The* Yann Barthès. Zena and I often watch his show, along with millions of people all over France. He's a big name in the media world. I don't hesitate for a moment.

"Of course, we'd be delighted. Do you want to film at our house?"

"No, Yann would like to interview you on set right away."

Quotidien with Yann Barthès! This is an incredible opportunity. A show with huge ratings, and we'll be given enough time to explain our situation at length, which hasn't been possible in my various interviews with M6, CNews, and France 3.

On December 1, Zena and I are in Paris for the show. We're very well looked after, pampered even, by the whole team, and Yann Barthès comes to see us in our dressing room to put us at ease before we step out onto the set, inevitably full of nerves. The journalist Martin Weill does an introductory piece, summarizing our story up to the point of the verdict, then Zena and I come on stage for the interview with Barthès. It lasts more than ten minutes and he lets us talk about our lives, about what we've been through since my arrest in Greece and—more particularly—since the recent trial and news of the verdict. I explain what drove me to go to Greece in the first place, our fear that my in-laws would drown on the crossing from Athens to Italy. Zena mentions the aspects of French law that we researched and that reassured us that no one was prosecuted for helping family members travel to or settle in France. She also describes the simplicity of our everyday lives, like so many other French families: No, we don't have the money we need to "buy" my freedom (and I still feel the same disgust at the concept) because we have children, a single salary, and a mortgage to pay. Who has thirteen thousand euros lying around these days?

This interview is a turning point in our mission to rally public opinion. In addition to giving us the time to express ourselves fully, the show puts our story in context with a montage of several reports on the migrant crisis in Greece and the Balkan states, and I'm grateful for this very relevant scene-setting. Crucially, though, our appearance on *Quotidien* produces an exponential rise not only in the number of signatures on the petition that we launched on Change.org in late October but also in the donations to the fund that we set up on Leetchi—a European GoFundMe. In three days we reach forty thousand signatures and the thirteen thousand euros we need to buy my freedom. I can't describe the happiness Zena and I feel, and this is naturally shared by both of our families. The French authorities may have been slow to come to my aid, but my fellow countrymen came forward swiftly and in great numbers. We're not alone. And the Greek justice system may not recognize my innocence, but the French people readily uphold it.

20

A reluctant appeal

The verdict does not come all of a sudden,
the proceedings gradually turn into the verdict.
—Franz Kafka, *The Trial*

On December 5, five days before the deadline for lodging an appeal, the Leetchi fund has reached the thirteen thousand euros that I must pay to the Greek Ministry of "Justice" (I think those quotation marks are essential) to avoid going to prison. I call Mrs. D.

"We've got the money together for the daily fine," I tell her. "Can you tell me how I make the payment?"

"I'll find out for you but don't forget there'll be legal costs to pay too."

"Yes, that's fine. How much are they?"

"I'll say this again, Mr. Pélissier: You should appeal, that's my advice."

"I'd rather close this chapter of my life, thanks. I'm not the only person concerned, I have a wife and two little girls, and they're deeply affected by what's going on, as you can imagine. We need to move on."

"As you wish. I'll go to the court to get the information you need and get back to you."

I relay this conversation to Zena over dinner. The legal costs will be a maximum of five hundred or a thousand euros—they never go above that sort of sum in France. We'll find a way to cover them ourselves.

The next day I receive an email from the lawyer with a scan of a document from the courts as an attachment. It is scrawled on by hand and partly illegible. It looks like a restaurant check, and, at first glance, my brain refuses to comprehend the total.

From: Christina D
Sent: Wednesday December 6, 2017 11:10
To: Stéphan Pélissier
Subject: Re: VERY URGENT TRIAL PATRAS

Dear Mr. Pélissier,

I spoke to the courts yesterday about the calculations for your sentence.

I'm attaching them here.

The sum of 14,052.50 euros relates to the Right to Increase.

At your service.

Christina D.

Attorney at Law

French Honorary Consul

I'm stunned, knocked sideways, incapable of assimilating this latest information. Yes, that really is what's written on the crumpled piece of paper that I keep studying incredulously. 14,000 euros on top of the 13,000 we were expecting to pay. In total, 27,676 euros, to be precise! How on earth can that be possible?

Nothing. Nothing logical about it, nothing fair, nothing acceptable, and nothing legitimate. A handwritten document for a legal ruling? A lawyer who can't tell us in advance the total sum we'll be required to pay? I'm reminded of the Syrian *courts and the things that discouraged me from practicing as a lawyer there. In order to succeed in the Syrian legal system, you first need to cultivate your network, preferably by sleeping with judges or other lawyers—something I always refused to do, obviously. As for defendants, it was very simple: They had to pay, slip bribes, and grease endless palms if they were to have any hope of getting out. I wanted to be a lawyer in a country that respects the law, and that's why I came to France. And now here I am going through this nightmare of corruption and arbitrary judgments with my husband.*

can barely control my anger when I call the lawyer.

"This must be a joke, Mrs. D., it's ridiculous! What the hell is this twenty-seven thousand euros?"

"There's the total for your daily fines and added to that is the Right to Increase, a law that was passed in 2007 to apply a tax of 110 percent to each day in prison converted to a daily fine."

"But you never mentioned this tax, and you obviously knew about it. Couldn't you have warned us about this as soon as you told me the verdict?"

"Well, I advised you to appeal. There's still time, but you'll need to be quick."

"But damn it, that's not what I'm asking you. Why didn't you tell us that we'd have to pay twenty-seven thousand euros instead of thirteen?"

"The situation is very clear, Mr. Pélissier: Either you pay the twenty-seven thousand euros to cover the daily fines plus the Right to Increase, or you appeal. It's December 7, you need to make up your mind. I'll wait to hear from you."

She hangs up, leaving me here with my anger and my questions. One thing's certain: This incompetent, hypocritical woman won't be my lawyer a moment longer.

Zena and I are really at our wits' end. We had completely believed it was all over. Now we'll be forced to appeal, and the four of us must continue living with this excruciating anxiety for many more months, perhaps years. And the shame! The shame in telling all those people—loved ones and anonymous strangers—who contributed to our fund. What to say, what to do? "Oops, so sorry, we got our numbers a little wrong, give us more money"? Totally unacceptable. We don't have time, anyway. With a very heavy heart, I give Mrs. D. one final instruction: She is to lodge an appeal in my name.

We must also—immediately—shut down the fund so that no one else can pay into it. I go online and receive a slap in the face: "Fund suspended for verification." I think I'm going crazy. What now?

I email the site's administrators and someone calls me back the next day to explain what's going on: A small far-right group has flagged our fund for violating French law.

As justification, they cite article 40 of an 1881 law: "No one may open or publicly announce a subscription fund intended to indemnify fines, expenses or damages handed down by legal sentencing in criminal or correctional proceedings, on pain of six months' imprisonment and a fine of 45,000 euros, or of one of these two penalties singly." The simple explanation for the fascist activists' sudden interest in the law is a number of recent convictions—in the name of this same article 40—of media personalities with links to the far right who appealed to the public when heavy fines were imposed on them. My appeal for donations therefore gives the extreme right a pretext to denounce me. It goes without saying that they're not happy with the idea of a Frenchman helping Syrians! The man who's called me is a key figure at Leetchi, and he's extremely embarrassed.

"You see," he says, "we've suspended several of their funds on this point of law in the past, which is why they now refer to procedural costs, and why they have this sort of crusade against anyone appealing for donations after legal entanglements. It was the only thing we could do with your fund. But at least now you know what to do: Change the name of your appeal for donations and we can unblock it within an hour."

I immediately alter the wording of the fund so that it doesn't refer to the daily fines; it's now for "legal fees and the cost of translating official documents." Which means that it's thanks to this fund that I can now hire a new lawyer, a highly qualified one this time, to defend me in my appeal. Leetchi keep to their word: The suspension is quickly lifted on the fund, and I close it down straightaway.

To dispel any doubts, I contact Éric Berger to get an article into *La Dépêche* as soon as possible. Zena and I apologize to all the donors and explain that the sum raised will be used to pay legal fees, translation costs, and expenses for the appeal hearing. If there is any money left after the appeal, we will split it equally between a charity that helps Syrians and one that helps homeless people in France. We're keen for this money to have a universal dimension because it was so generously given to us by thousands of people.

I now need to prepare for this new trial and set up my defense with a different lawyer...but most of all I must support my family and be there for Zena and the girls. I really hope the appeal takes place soon; we can't cope with years of this worrying, with this sword of Damocles over our heads.

21.

Being French!

ZENA'S STORY

So you're from Syria? That's great. Are you happy in France? And you don't miss home too much?"

Home? But this is my home. Here in Albi. The town where I live, where I've built a house with my French husband, where my French daughters were born and go to school...

But it's true, Damascus is also home... It was until the war meant I couldn't stay there, and I still used to spend three weeks' holiday there every year after I left to study in France. It was always so wonderful to see my family again. Some of my happiest memories are of enjoying tabbouleh and *fattoush* with my sister Mirvat amid the smell of roses and jasmine in the inner courtyard of a typical restaurant. We'd go there to recharge our batteries after spending a long morning happily getting lost in the arcades and laby-rinthine passageways of the big covered bazaar. My sister was much better at bargaining than I was, and we had fun comparing our acquisitons over lunch.

Yes, I've been naturalized at last, but I still don't have the stability of a regular job and I don't have that inte-grated feeling of someone who spends time every day with coworkers. I haven't really been subjected to discrimina-tion but I've faced casual racism in the form of disparag-ing remarks about my country, particularly while I was studying in France. There were little comments like, "Yes, but standards aren't so high there..." Still, I managed to get a master's in French law, and I've almost finished my thesis, but these comments had a powerful effect on me because I'm always questioning my own merits.

In any event, I can make the most of my life now that I live in France—especially now that my parents are safely here too. I think of my family members who stayed in Syria and I know their circumstances are very differ-ent: my grandmother who's sick and struggles to access the care she needs; my cousin who died in 2013 because in a war-torn country you can easily die of blood loss; and aunts and uncles who are forced to donate funds to the regime just to ensure their own safety. And yes, I was a lawyer, teaching at law school...but I was in a coun-try with no democracy and no freedom of expression, and we hardly even realized because we'd grown up in that world since our earliest childhood. In the 1980s one of my grandfathers, who was a reasonably well-known poet, was denounced as a dissident and he disappeared overnight. My family didn't try to find him, it was pointless, we knew without really knowing. Four years later he turned up out of the blue on a public garbage dump; he was completely naked, diabetic, almost blind, and he'd lost his mind in captivity. His children did everything they could to care for him until he died shortly after returning home. The family discussed this with no one, not even close friends.

I don't forget about my origins: Syria will always be in my heart, and I'm keen to pass on my language and culture to my daughters, despite my new nationality. But at the end of the day, I want to live in France, now and forever, as a Frenchwoman. Which is why I wanted to be naturalized as soon as possible. It took eleven years...

When I'd spent five years on French soil I thought I'd be able to apply for citizenship straightaway in 2012, but the answer came back that the time spent studying didn't count because I had married in the meantime: I could now apply after four years of marriage. Until then I would have to renew my residence permit every year. When I renewed it in 2012, new legislation had come into effect and I had an interview with the OFII to present my case, explain my professional status, and have my familiarity with the French language assessed. I was already bilingual by then so the interview stopped there, but French lessons were set up for other immigrants and these became compulsory if people wanted their residence permits renewed. I also had to attend a compulsory training day in Albi about civil rights in France.

Just before Mila's birth, in the summer of 2016, I go to the prefecture in Albi determined to apply for French citizenship because I have now been married for four years. At this point I'm told that citizenship services have been "centralized" so I must go to Toulouse. But appointments are made online and every time I go onto the site, I get the message "No more appointments currently available." I check again as often as possible, two or three times a day, sometimes more. It's always the same.

Four months.

It takes me four months to secure an appointment.

Four months at a rate of three or four attempts a day.

In preparation for the interview, I start collecting the necessary documents, some of which need to be sent from Syria, which is always very complicated and expensive.

In November 2016 Stéphan, Mila, and I make the journey to the prefectural office and I watch nervously as the woman handling my application silently scrutinizes all the documents I've supplied.

"I can't see the marriage certificate for your first marriage, Mrs. Pélissier..."

"No, but I've got the relevant divorce papers, look."

"Yes, but I need the marriage certificate. This means your application's incomplete so I won't register it. Come back when you've got everything you need."

I mumble a goodbye and stalk out of her office, furious. What's the point of asking for a marriage certificate for a marriage that's over? Surely what matters is that I'm not married to two people at once? Either way, I know I won't have the last word on this so I manage to track down the certificate, at a cost of nearly two hundred euros. Then I spend another three months trying to get my next appointment before returning to the prefectural office, alone this time, in March 2017.

The appointment gets off to a bad start; the woman dealing with my application is extremely unpleasant. She flicks very quickly through my file—she's clearly done this a lot.

"There's a document missing."

"What? No! There can't be, I checked ten times!"

"Listen, I know my job. Your Syrian police clearance certificate isn't here."

But it was there at my previous appointment... I can feel the blood draining from my face. Yes, I took it out of the folder when I reorganized everything into chronological order. I must have left it on my desk. The strain's too much for me, I break down and cry.

"I can't take this anymore, your online appointment system is driving me crazy! It'll take me months to get another appointment."

And then there's a miracle: the woman on the other side of the desk becomes a human being.

"I understand. Everyone has the same problem, you know. Listen, as an exception I'll give you my email address. Once your file's complete, message me and I'll see you as soon as possible."

Let's hope the third time's the charm! I'm seen by the same woman in early April, and this time she's all smiles and even confides in me a little about her own story—because it turns out she too has been naturalized. She registers my application and warns me that it may take a long time to process.

A few weeks later I get a phone call at two o'clock on a Thursday afternoon.

"Mrs. Pélissier? This is Thierry M. of the national police force. I will be with you in an hour for an inspection with regard to your application for French citizenship."

The police officer arrives in civilian dress and explains that he needs to inspect our home to check that our marriage isn't a front. Luckily, the officer and I realize immediately that we know each other because I recently applied to work as a sworn translator and had an interview at the police precinct. This is just as well because it's normally not a good thing for one half of the couple to be out of the house... but this is a weekday afternoon so my husband's at work, like most people, wouldn't you think? Thierry M. tells me that he usually inspects the bedroom and bathroom but in our case he'll settle for letting me tell our story over a cup of coffee.

It took another year but it's now done: I've officially been French since August 2018. I still have my original nationality and in my heart I have a double feeling of pride—I'm Syrian *and* French.

22.

Today and tomorrow . . .

t is late 2018 and my father-in-law, mother-in-law, Anas, and Mayada now live together in an apartment in a housing project in Joué-lès-Tours.

Saif Eddine wants to become a bus driver and already has the equivalent of the relevant qualification thanks to the heavy goods vehicle license that he obtained in the Syrian army. All that's missing now is competence in the French language, so he's diligently attending French lessons. He's a very active member of the small local Syrian community, always ready to help people out, especially with home improvements, which are his passion. According to Anas and Mayada, he's completely changed since settling in France: He's much more relaxed about everything, and particularly about when and how often they're allowed out. In Damascus, he was always afraid something terrible would happen to one of his children; in France he knows that he and his family are safe. The only thing missing is a feeling of some standing in society, and that's something a proper job would give him.

Wafaa speaks very good French, much better than her husband's, and she too really wants to find work. If she's to achieve this she'll need to overcome her natural reserve, and she's increasingly enthusiastic about the idea of working in catering, in a canteen maybe... after all she so loves cooking for other people! She's admitted to her daughter that, even though she misses the scents of Damascus, she does really value how peaceful her life feels in France. Back in Syria she was terribly restricted by oppressive conventions and other people's judgmental gossip. She doesn't have to play a game of appearances here and doesn't live in constant fear of being judged.

Mayada still has serious health problems that mean she can't work. She has undergone several operations for her pancreatitis but it's not over yet. Sadly, she is probably the one who's having the toughest time: She used to be a legal expert at the Ministry of Transport and had a busy social life, but now her prospects are reduced to medical treatments and the strict diet she must follow. Although she misses Syria, of course, it's really her illness that's hampering her progress.

Anas has made his big sister Zena so proud: Now that his father no longer feels he must watch over him all the time, Anas is free to demonstrate what a dazzling young man he is. He's made friends and always manages to be kind and humorous when confronted with prejudice; he's trilingual and shows true excellence in his engineering studies and at chess; and he's hoping to become a computer engineer.

Mirvat, who came to France in October 2016, now also has political refugee status, and she lives and works in Joué-lès-Tours.

Meanwhile, Samer stayed in Castres when the rest of Zena's family moved to the Loiret region. At the end of tenth grade he decided to train as a cook in Castres. He's very excited about his work prospects, and my parents-in-law still keep an eye on him long distance. As a minor he was entitled to have his own family with him, but the process took too long and stopped dead as soon as he turned eighteen, so his mother is still stuck in Syria, where she has a very tough life because she has extremely limited resources. Samer is doing everything he can to secure a visa for her that would allow her to apply for asylum in France.

Zena and I work hard at continuing to support the cause of refugees—we feel it's very important not to think only of ourselves. Sure, we have busy schedules like anyone else, what with work, Julia and Mila, and everything we need to do to prepare for the appeal and maintain the profile of our case. And, like many French people, our finances are often tight.

I personally pass on huge amounts of information on social media to inform my followers; and I ask people to sign petitions and offer support to movements or individuals who help migrants, people such as Laurent Caffier and Cédric Herrou. Every now and then we donate clothes to the charity Emmaüs or send tarpaulins to Calais (refugees need them to shelter from bad weather and, unfortunately, they need a lot of them because the tarps are often torn up by hostile gangs or stolen by selfish profiteers who then resell them). Whenever I can, I also publicize events that will encourage people to make donations: I contributed to a day organized by Réseau Education Sans Frontières (RESF, a network committed to "education without borders"), and Zena and I responded to an appeal by an organization called La Parlote that was running a Syrian evening at a literary café near where we live. It was a wonderful opportunity for people of all ages and from all walks of life to meet, and the donations raised were given to Syria Charity, a responsible and well-run NGO that really does make a difference in Syria. It is active in a number of fields, offering food, medical supplies, and security, as well as sponsoring and giving regular support to 6,500 orphans. Zena and I also give a modest monthly donation to Doctors Without Borders in order to contribute to its humanitarian work all over the world. After what happened to her parents when they asked for political asylum,

Zena also likes to offer her legal expertise to refugees: She helps foreigners with their research, their applications, and sourcing of documents, sometimes working pro bono when the refugees have no funds.

Zena and I signed up for and participated in an ECI (European Citizens' Initiative) called "We are a welcoming Europe": We were included in a series of film portraits of people who, like us, had legal problems after helping refugees in distress for no personal profit. Other subjects of these portraits include Cédric Herrou, Martine Landry, Rob Lawrie, Pierre-Alain Mannoni, and Francesca Peirotti. As I finish writing this book, I don't know whether this ECI film will succeed in its aim of being viewed by the European Commission...but I sincerely hope it does.

23.

The fight goes on

t isn't until June 2018 that I'm notified of the date of my appeal: It will be heard on March 1, 2019. Of course, I have continued to be active since I was first sentenced. I know that, whatever happens, I mustn't disappear off the media radar... or the political radar.

As soon as I know the date for my new trial I activate my loyal network of supportive journalists, and the information is spread far and wide through *La Dépêche du Midi*, France 3, and, thanks to Maxime Macé, *France-Soir*. Other media outlets go for more in-depth profiles, rather than reporting in the heat of the moment. In July 2018 *l'Humanité* devotes a long article by Émilien Urbach to the case. I was put in touch with Émilien by the man often referred to as "the Zorro of the Calais Jungle,"

Laurent Caffier, who I met through social media; I was impressed by the tenacity with which he does whatever he can to help refugees on a daily basis.

Laurent Caffier has also been prosecuted for helping three Iranians to flee France in 2016, even though he did this for no financial gain. The three men were among the *"bouches cousues"* (sealed lips), a group of twelve refugees who stitched up their own lips live in front of TV cameras and mics in their appeal for help: They wanted to go to England but were stuck in the notorious Calais Jungle refugee camp. Three of them had tried and failed to go via Spain and were then held prisoner by their smuggler. They miraculously managed to escape, and it was at this point that Laurent picked them up, in very poor health. He took them into his own home, with his family, and ended up in a stalemate: He couldn't ask them to go back to the Jungle because their smuggler would find them and kill them. Nor could he take them to the police precinct because they were undocumented immigrants; they would have been sent back to Iran where they would have been executed for fleeing the country. He had only one option: To help them get out. So he decided to find a boat that would take them to England. When I met Laurent, he was waiting for his appeal hearing, having been found guilty in June 2017 of "aiding illegal entry and residency," and convicted with no specific sentence announced. After the appeal in 2018, he received a suspended six-month prison sentence.

Like me, Laurent acted for no personal profit. Like me, he's fighting to shine a spotlight on this sort of conviction as an affront to basic human solidarity. He powerfully asserts his sheer humanity and his inability to walk on by when he sees someone suffering. I have huge respect for his commitment and courage.

After Zena and I appeared on Yann Barthès's show, several publishing companies contacted us offering book deals, and that's how you come to be reading this today. It's my dearest wish that this book will open up discussions at a European—perhaps global—level on the need to standardize immigration legislation and on how we view and handle the distress of exiles. Countless anonymous individuals help refugees and take substantial risks in the process, threatened by the law as much as by far-right factions. Many people who know us would like to help but don't dare take the plunge because of the risks involved. But this help wouldn't simply be welcome, it's absolutely indispensable. There are thousands of refugees in great distress in France, and the people who want to help them out of simple generosity should be able to do so without fear. Solidarity can't be—*mustn't* be—an offense.

Staying visible and maintaining a presence in the collective subconscious—these are vital.

Because I'm dreading the outcome of this appeal.

In May 2018 I finally receive the documents that explain my conviction in November 2017. Of course they are in Greek, and when I have them translated I'm devastated.

First of all, one of the police officers who arrested us and held us in custody (I'll never know which one) claimed in his statement that I never mentioned that the passengers in my car were members of my family.

Most significantly, I discover that, contrary to the information given to me by my lawyer, I wasn't facing up to nine years in prison, but fifteen! This is because the Greek judicial system can allocate a three-year sentence for each refugee that the accused has helped.

Lastly, I gather that a sentence cannot always be converted into daily fines. So Zena was right: It all depends on what the defendant looks like, and I look like a Frenchman, which, as far as the Greeks are concerned, means I can afford to pay.

The good news is that Zena and I have found a new lawyer whom we really trust. Mr. Kerasiotis has a lot of experience in cases like ours. He is a member of the Human Rights League and has already defended cases at the European Court of Human Rights. He was also instrumental in the first marriage between two Syrians in a refugee camp in Greece. Zena and I have a lot of faith in him. Since he took over our case, he's been very communicative and has advised me not to relax for a moment with my media campaign because he too believes it's a crucial form of support.

I know that I'm not obligated to appear before the court for the appeal hearing so I've asked whether it would be appropriate for me to be there. He's looking into this but will suggest it only if there's absolutely no risk—only if he's quite sure that I will be able to get out of Greece after the trial, whatever the outcome. Because he's warned me that if we do succeed in securing an appeal, it would not be suspensive, and it goes without saying that I refuse to spend so much as a minute in a Greek prison.

I remember what I tweeted the day before the original trial: "Should we impose legal sanctions on actions that are not morally reprehensible?"

Truth be told, I don't think I'll ever return to Greece, and this is a particularly bitter assertion for me to make when I remember my grandmother Voula Paraskevi and the country where I once had strong ties and wonderful memories. After my grandmother died, I traveled to Crete with my parents and my sister; none of us had been there before but we suddenly felt a need to visit. My mother in particular wanted to reestablish links with her family, including her cousin Nikos, who'd never left the island. We instantly fell in love with its Middle Eastern way of life, a sweet simple existence where it takes just tomatoes, bread, cheese, and olive oil to share the most wonderful meal as you look out over the sea . . . that meeting with Nikos was magical for me. He is a wise, gentle, and cultured polyglot who cultivates a beautiful form of freedom far removed from the frenzy of this world. I've lost count of the hours I spent talking with him, putting the world to rights until the sun came up . . . so long as we had souvlaki and cigarettes, there was no stopping us. I was in my thirties and I had an urge to leave behind my French life and move to Crete, but Nikos helped me understand that this environment of happiness and well-being is something we carry within us and can build wherever we choose. I took great pleasure in introducing him to Zena just after we were married, but we haven't returned to Crete since the girls were born—I would so love them to meet him. After what happened in Patras, though, we need to face the facts: It will never happen. And that makes me very sad.

In the end—and I'm sure it's down to pressure from the media and the public—the French authorities may actually make a difference to my appeal hearing.

After I wrote to the French president, I eventually received a reply from Nathalie Loiseau, the minister for European affairs, just after Christmas 2017.

MINISTRY FOR EUROPE AND FOREIGN AFFAIRS

The Minister
Responsible for European Affairs
Paris, December 26, 2017

[text redacted]

Dear sir,

Your letter has reached the President of the Republic who has instructed me to reply to you.

I'm moved to hear of your situation relating to the crisis affecting the Syrian people and the personal crises experienced by your in-laws in fleeing the war.

I gather that you have been able to assert your rights, on the one hand thanks to the advice of our honorary consul in Patras who is a lawyer by profession and is helping you with the Greek legal process, and on the other hand by appealing against the decision reached by the court in Patras.

It is not appropriate for me to comment on a court's decision, nor to intervene in an on-going legal process. While respecting these limitations, I apprised my Greek counterpart, Georgios KATROUGALOS, of your situation during the last meeting of the General Council in Brussels on December 12. He is well aware how baffling it will appear to the French public.

This matter is all the more sensitive because, although it is a crime to assist illegal immigrants in France, French law allows an exception in the case of family members.

. . . / . . .

While we wait for a ruling on your appeal, the Ministry for Europe and Foreign Affairs and, more specifically, our consulate in Athens are of course mobilized to help you defend your rights.

Yours sincerely,

Nathalie LOISEAU

Mr. Stéphan PÉLISSIER
[text redacted]

MAILING ADDRESS: 37 Quai d'Orsay 75700 Paris 07 SP—SWITCHBOARD: 01 43 17 53 53

This letter with its talk of "mobilization" when I'd just faced such a resounding conviction felt almost ironic. But everything went into overdrive in the summer of 2018. Senator Bonnecarrère, who has followed my case from the start, had a meeting with me in his office to be brought up to date about my situation and to inform me that a representative of the French consulate could attend the appeal trial. This is extraordinary news, if it actually happens. The problem is France has only a little room for maneuvering in its efforts to help me. Greece is a sovereign state and as such it must be allowed to carry out its legal proceedings perfectly independently. If the French consulate sends a representative to attend my trial, the message will be both subtle and clear: France is giving the defendant her support and standing by his side. There is no offense in that to Greece, the court will acknowledge it without taking exception.

Naturally, I immediately discussed this with Zena but we didn't want to celebrate too soon, not before we were sure. Luckily, we have received assurances on this point since then.

In early November 2017, just before the trial, my co-worker Alexandre O. put me in contact with José Bové who is a member of the European Parliament. His response was as swift as it was heartfelt: He officially stood up in my favor and, in our various exchanges, asked me to give him regular updates through his parliamentary attaché, Anne L. And so, after my meeting with the senator, I contacted her to discuss this possible support from the consulate. She then decided to ask José Bové to write to Nathalie Loiseau for official confirmation. On August 3, 2018, José Bové received this confirmation that Anne L. immediately forwarded to us.

MINISTRY FOR EUROPE AND FOREIGN AFFAIRS

The Minister
Responsible for European Affairs
Paris, August 03, 2018

[text redacted]

Dear sir,

Thank you for your letter drawing my attention to the circumstances of Mr. Stéphan Pélissier whose verdict for his appeal hearing in Greece has been set for March 1, 2019.

I am very familiar with our fellow countryman's circumstances, and with the services of the Ministry for Europe and Foreign Affairs, in both Paris and Athens.

Even though Mr. Pélissier is in France, attendance at the legal proceedings concerning him can indeed be assured in collaboration with the lawyer defending his interests.

Our official is in regular contact with the French Embassy in Athens, who will send a representative to attend the appeal trial.

I have also informed my Greek counterpart of the feelings aroused in France by Mr. Pélissier's situation,

which we are still following with considerable
vigilance.

Yours sincerely,

Nathalie LOISEAU

Mr. José BOVÉ
Member of the European Parliament
Montredon
[text redacted]

MAILING ADDRESS: 37 Quai d'Orsay 75700
Paris 07 SP—SWITCHBOARD: 01 43 17 53 53
WEB ADDRESS: www.diplomatie.gouv.fr.

As a way of further expanding my file (the more political content it has the better it will look to the Greek
legal system), I've written to Nathalie Loiseau again to say
that I've duly noted her support and the attendance of the
consulate whatever the circumstances, even if the trial is
postponed. I'm hoping for a reply from her.

sometimes look back—with amusement—at the life I once
lived, the certainties I had, the life I led before... Before I

met Zena and got to know her family. Before I was aware of the harrowing circumstances that drive whole families to climb into already punctured boats and attempt crossings that they believe are not as dangerous as living in their home country. Before I learned, from my in-laws' experiences, how these desperate people who've already lost everything are treated in France. Ten years ago I had a number of prejudices about undocumented immigrants, about foreigners and their reasons for coming to France, and I sometimes thought that disadvantaged people didn't always put in enough effort to dig themselves out of their situations. I now know that leaving your homeland is a tragic decision, I understand the terrible difficulties encountered along the way, the life-threatening risks that these people run at every moment, the horrors of coming up against incomprehensible laws in rich countries that seem so capable of taking you in, but just don't. People tell me this, and I know it's true: I've really changed, and the way I see things has changed. And this is just as obvious in my private life as it is in my work, where I now favor the human element in every situation.

Doing everything I can to maintain a strong media profile. Alerting the authorities and securing every possible form of support. Getting people to rally around us. That's what my life has become, that's what our lives have become for many months now. Zena and I are not in the least heroic or extraordinary. We're ordinary people who've ended up in a form of torment that's way beyond us, but we won't let it get the better of us. There are periods of euphoria when I feel the stars have aligned in our favor, and times of deep despondency when I think the appeal will only add to my sentence. And then in those dark hours there's always something, and sometimes it's almost insignificant, that allows me to pull myself together and find the energy to continue fighting to have my innocence recognized in the eyes of the law. It might be the communal strength of all the activists battling to ensure that refugees in France are treated humanely; or the strangers, the people who send us simple anonymous messages of support on social media, or stop us in the street or at the supermarket checkout to tell us they're with us; our friends who surround us with their unfailing affection; and our family, of course. On our wedding day, Zena and I started building this family with my parents, my sister, her parents, sisters, and brother. And our two young daughters are its crowning glory. Of course, this whole saga has created tensions, some of them unbearable, but we've held out, we've stood up to them, and I'm enormously grateful for the feeling of family solidarity around us. Because that's exactly what I felt when I set off for Greece to stop Saif, Wafaa, Mimo, Anas, and Samer from going to their certain deaths. As I finish this book, I don't know what the Greek court will decide at my appeal. But whatever happens, a whole family will be united in confronting its decision. And, as they say, *Inshallah!*

Afterword

t is Friday, March 1, 2019. I'm with my wife, Zena, at Orly Airport, Paris. It's around midday.

We're waiting to board a flight to Toulouse to meet up with my parents and, more importantly, our two little girls, Julia and Mila.

We've just had an intense week of press interviews and television appearances for the publication of our book. It was meant to be published sooner, in the hope of generating a lot of media interest. In the end, it came out yesterday. Still, we did manage to send a copy to our Greek lawyers so they could add it to the file.

After the shock of finding myself sentenced, in November 2017, to seven years in prison with no possibility of parole, and the continuing long legal nightmare, this book felt like a self-evident necessity. We needed to free ourselves from the emotional weight accumulated over the years of this ordeal by laying it to rest on paper.

We feel it is a genuine firsthand account of present-day French society, and one with particular resonance in the context of our contemporary world, because it addresses questions such as exile, the experiences of refugees, the criminalization of solidarity, the inability of European leaders to tackle the biggest migration crisis since World War II, and the need to reform the UN's operational regulations.

We also needed to record what had happened. To describe how in Europe, in our time, you can be treated as a criminal, like someone who has stolen or killed, when you have only tried to save people; and in my case, my family, who were fleeing a dictatorship and ISIS.

During the initial trial in 2017, the criminal courts in Patras sentenced me to seven years of prison without parole for the mass transportation of undocumented immigrants in Greece in 2015. To put it plainly, I was seen as just another people smuggler, even though the immigrants concerned were members of my family.

In France, anyone who has directly or indirectly facilitated or attempted to facilitate a foreigner's illegal entry into, travel within, or residency in the country is punishable by law.

But that same law does not apply when there is a family connection between the perpetrator and the illegal immigrant.

Theoretically, then, I was not risking legal proceedings in France. But what about Greece? Even though Greece is a member of the European Union, and the union's member states are meant to standardize their laws, I had no idea what would happen to me if we were stopped. And that doubt was my constant companion over a journey of more than 2,500 kilometers. The day before I left, I'd searched in vain for the applicable Greek measures in such a situation, to see whether the regulations were the same as in France. But the legal information was all in Greek and online translations were completely incomprehensible. I therefore decided to travel to Greece and bring back my in-laws without being sure what risks I was running. At worst, I thought I would be fined, but would never have envisioned being arrested, held in custody in conditions worthy of the Soviet Union, and—worse still—given a seven-year prison sentence.

This punishment was wholly out of proportion to the deed. In France, you might be imprisoned for several years for a "crime of passion" murder. The sentences for rape are lower than the one handed down to me; sometimes there is even a reprieve for sex attacks. So seven years with no parole when I hadn't stolen, raped, or killed was, in both personal and legal terms, an aberration and a scandal.

But make no mistake, this book is also and primarily a love story. It is a testimony to the strength that love can bring to bear in your actions by giving you the courage to surpass yourself and do things you would never have achieved without it—in short, to sacrifice yourself, in a manner of speaking.

When I met Zena I immediately embraced Syrian culture, which was so close to the Greek culture I inherited from my grandmother. Zena often made culinary specialties for me, and within a few months, I gained ten pounds. I started to learn a few words of Syrian so that I could communicate with her family. We used to listen to the Lebanese singer Fairuz, and Zena gave me nostalgic descriptions of Damascus, the oldest city in the world.

But ever since that first meeting, I was also thrown headlong into the Syrian civil war. The peaceful revolution for freedom began in the very early days of our idyll. I started following some Syrian activists on social networks. There were harrowing eyewitness accounts and documentaries, tortured civilians, children who were skeletal or had had limbs amputated.

For those Syrians, as it was for my father-in-law, leaving their country was the hardest decision to make. It really was heartbreaking. But new dangers, threats to their families and the advances made by ISIS, often left them with no choice. What would we have done in their situation? Most likely the same as my parents-in-law, the same thing that millions of people have done through the ages in order to escape abject poverty or war.

France has a long tradition of taking in immigrants, whether they are fleeing hunger, war, or dictatorships. Every French person can count among his or her friends or relations a grandparent from Spain, Italy, Portugal, Poland, or Africa.

Our identity is built on this multicultural heritage and, in spite of this, nothing has really changed: Immigrants are never made welcome. Particularly in times of economic crisis, when they are always used as scapegoats. They are rejected, discriminated against, imprisoned, and—in the worst instances—subjected to violence, or even openly killed, as happened recently on the Greek–Turkish border.

Tens of thousands of refugees, including many children, are crammed into camps in Hungary, Greece, Lebanon, and Turkey. They live with danger, are vulnerable to viruses, and develop poor mental health. And that's when they're not being bombarded on the Turkish–Syrian border by the army of Bashar al-Assad's regime and its Russian allies, watched silently by Western leaders.

Since 2019 far-right populist parties have achieved the highest rankings in the European elections in France.

Zena's brother, Anas, who is following a higher education course in information technology, desperately wishes people would change the way they think of refugees. He often talks about Steve Jobs, who also has Syrian roots— "He's my role model," Anas tells me.

From the moment we woke up this morning, March 1, 2019, a few hours before the verdict is due, Zena and I have been in a state of anxiety. Today is of paramount importance to us and our family. Because on this day my second trial before the Patras criminal court opens near Athens in Greece. One thing I know already is that, whatever the verdict, it will definitely be implemented, because any appeal would not be suspensive: So it will be prison or freedom.

But what exactly is my crime? I didn't steal. I didn't rape. I didn't kill.

On the eve of my first trial in 2017, I put this question on my Twitter feed. It was the only question that needed to be asked: "Should we impose legal sanctions on actions that are not morally reprehensible?"

As we sit side by side in the airport departure lounge, there's a palpable tension. Zena gets up to buy some macaroons. There's a shop right in front of us. We'll have them later with the girls.

I leaf absentmindedly through a magazine, perhaps hoping to find something else to think about. But my thoughts are elsewhere. I'm going back over the key events since that day in August 2015 when my life was about to change. People aren't usually aware of that moment, of that schism after which things will never be the same.

We've waited more than eighteen months for this trial. Life, routine, and everyday concerns have regained the upper hand. Even though somewhere in the backs of our minds, the threat of a second prison sentence has always lurked.

We forget about it most of the time. But it's when we catch ourselves daydreaming, daring to hope . . . that's when the threat rears its head. It was there all along, hidden, skulking in a shady corner of our subconscious. Waiting for the right moment when our guard was down.

Until the end of 2018, I was a legal officer at a large French company. Confronted with the prospect of another trial in 2019, I lost my appetite for most things. I couldn't find much meaning in my work, or my life. All my thoughts and energies were focused on that deadline.

2019 was one of the most important years of our lives. I left my job with absolutely no prospects of employment, we published this book, and the long-awaited appeal hearing took place on March 1.

It's midday. My cell vibrates. I have some WhatsApp messages. It's my lawyer. I can't believe my eyes. He tells me we've won. My 2017 sentence to seven years' imprisonment has quite simply been overturned, quashed. I'm released. My lawyer will later admit that the appeal court's reasoning did not take into account international tracts on the rights of refugees, but that we won on a point of procedure. Greece would not want an overly favorable decision to send a positive signal to refugees' families—who might be tempted to come and collect their immigrating relatives on Greek soil—because in 2015 there were 2,000 to 3,000 refugees a day flooding into the Greek isles. But the technicalities don't matter—we've won! My sentence has been quashed. I'm released.

Zena and I hug. She's crying, she can't breathe. We kiss again and again. Surrounded by people laughing at us!

It's over, the nightmare is at an end. We never really dared to believe it would be. Having been burned so badly at the first trial. We call our parents. There's a feeling of unbounded euphoria. And of a weight suddenly being lifted.

I feel as if I'm waking from a very long nightmare. And for the first time in a long while I feel free, unfettered. The oppression has gone. A completely new sensation.

We must savor this moment, record these emotions, remember these images, so that we can keep replaying them and enjoy them again and again in the future.

I will make my final television appearance this evening. I've been invited onto the daily regional news show *France 3 Occitanie.* I've kept this news exclusively for them and a handful of print journalists who have become friends because, right from the very beginning, like thousands of people all over France, they believed in us.

But we're already in a hurry to turn this page, to get back to normal life, to a serene, regular existence, with our loved ones and our friends.

And now, more than a year later, on April 23, 2020, all that is behind us.

Zena and I have been profoundly changed by this whole experience.

We have sold our house and left the south of France to move north. We needed a change of scenery.

Zena has become a translator and interpreter at the law courts in Lille, near Paris. I have moved into trade unionism, working as a legal manager, perhaps to throw myself into different battles.

The crime of solidarity has now been mitigated in France, and luckily there are no longer legal proceedings against "any natural or legal person, when the offending act did not give rise to any direct or indirect compensation and consisted of providing legal, linguistic, or social advice or support, or any other aid offered with exclusively humanitarian intentions."

But what is the situation in Greece? And the rest of Europe?

Sometimes I wake in the middle of the night in a sweat. Images and emotions from my arrest resurface. I occasionally have panic attacks, I feel as if I can't breathe. Then I remember it's all over, it all ended well. And I can go back to sleep.

I also think back to that evening near Athens in 2015, when I shared a hotel bedroom with Zena's brother, Anas, and her cousin Samer. We came up with a jokey nickname for ourselves that evening, it was our way of recording the absurdity of the situation, our little note of sarcasm and irony: We called ourselves the "good criminals."

Acknowledgments

Zena and I would like to extend our heartfelt thanks to everyone who has given us support in any way, be they family, friends, loved ones, neighbors, acquaintances, strangers... It's thanks to you that we had the strength to keep going despite the obstacles, never giving up hope. Your acts of kindness, both great and small, comforted and strengthened us in our fight, and warmed our hearts when the road ahead looked dark. To all of you, and there are so many of you: Thank you!

Thank you also to Éditions Michel Lafon and especially Margaux Mersié, Maïte Ferracci-Buffiere, and Cécile-Agnès Champart for their unfailing faith in us and for their support.

Appendices

The Dublin III Regulation

When my parents-in-law ran the risk of being deported to Hungary, it was because they had been "dublinned," and this is an explanation of exactly what that means.

The Dublin III Regulation is in fact the nickname given to ruling number 604-2013 that was made by the European Parliament and the European Council on June 26, 2013. The text of this ruling, which was signed by the member states of the European Union along with Switzerland, Iceland, Norway, and Liechtenstein, delegates responsibility for examining refugees' requests for asylum to the first country in which they arrive. In other words, it isn't refugees themselves who choose where they want to ask for asylum, but the vagaries of their journey and their specific point of entry into Europe that decide for them.

So migrants who reach Europe via Italy and are registered in that country—either willingly or by force—would not be able to ask for asylum in France even if that is their wish and even if they succeed in reaching France. Thanks to fingerprint files that are shared on the Eurodac computer network among all the signatories to the regulation, when refugees' applications are registered at a French prefecture, they would automatically be subject to the "Dublin procedure" and risk being sent back to their country of entry, in this example Italy, which has the sovereign right to handle their request for asylum. One third of the 120,000 requests for asylum made in France in 2017 were subject to the Dublin procedure, and more than 4,000 people were deported to their country of entry. There are, however, possible exceptions and dispensations: reuniting families takes precedence over the ruling, and asylum seekers can submit pleas if they feel they're at risk of being mistreated in their country of entry—these were among the arguments that we used to defend my parents-in-law, very legitimately in view of the horrors that they suffered in Hungary, which was their point of entry.

In an attempt to justify the spirit of this regulation, which has been criticized ever since it was first signed, the European Union argues that asylum seekers will be given the same treatment and the same reception in all member states, and asserts that the explicit aim of Dublin III is to ensure that asylum seekers' cases are handled swiftly. In actual fact, each individual state is perfectly autonomous in its decision whether—or not—to grant asylum, and many outspoken detractors denounce the differences in how these applications are handled in the various countries within the Union.

The 2015 migrant crisis, with its huge rise in refugee numbers and the chaotically inconsistent way they were handled in different European countries, highlighted the controversy surrounding Dublin III. At the time, a number of countries decided unilaterally to suspend the application of the regulation: Germany stopped deporting all refugees who had been dublinned in Greece because Athens—which, along with Italy, is the main point of entry into Europe—could no longer handle refugees or their applications appropriately. At Germany's instigation, quotas were established as a matter of urgency for distributing asylum seekers among the different member states. But this Europe-wide decision was not respected in many countries, including France, which took in only four thousand people of its quota of thirty thousand. To their exasperation, Italy and Greece still stood alone on the front line.

When, in March 2016, Greece applied pressure to have its burden of migrants alleviated, the European Union eventually signed a barbaric accord with Turkey with the intention of reducing the influx of refugees. By the terms of this accord, Turkey undertakes to stop (or at least greatly reduce) migrations into Europe, and agrees that migrants who cross the Turkish–Greek border can be deported back onto Turkish soil. By way of compensation, the EU pledged to lift restrictions on visas granted to Turks for entering the Schengen area. But that's not all: Three crucial points in the accord put human rights organizations on red alert. Firstly, the accord provides for different treatment in the case of Syrians: Of those eligible to seek asylum, the number allowed into EU territory will equal the number of Syrians deported back to Turkey, and will be capped at 72,000 individuals a year—an upper limit set to suit Hungary's wishes. Secondly, this accord inevitably has advantageous financial implications for Turkey, which had essentially found itself a good strategy as a frontier-guard whose effectiveness was guaranteed by its brutality: The release of a previously established three-billion-euro fund would be accelerated to compensate Turkey for the costs incurred in abiding by the accord, and a new three-billion-euro fund would be handed over if Turkey honored its commitments effectively. Lastly, the accord also allowed for preliminary discussions about Turkey becoming a member of the EU, even though many defenders of human rights pointed out that Turkey's membership would be completely at odds with the principles of the Union.

Following the signing of this accord, Italy became the first point of entry for refugees, a situation that—stoked by the far right—fueled the anger of the Italian people and facilitated the rise to power of former deputy prime minister Matteo Salvini and his supporters in June 2018.

Reforms to the Dublin III regulation have been under discussion since 2016, but no consensus has been reached, particularly on the question of quotas. Charities remain on the alert about these talks, especially because one option being discussed is the deportation of asylum seekers into a non-EU "third-party" country through which they have traveled if that country is deemed "safe": Reading between the lines, this would give long-term ratification to the migrant-related accords established between the EU and Turkey.

While Europe struggles to agree on a shared migrant policy, tens of thousands of refugees are stuck in an administrative dead end and a humanitarian crisis. Migrants are forced into appalling conditions in overpopulated camps on Greek islands, referred to as "hot spots" in official documents. In Moria, a "hot spot" on the island of Lesbos, a facility intended for three thousand people currently accommodates nine thousand, one third of them children. In concrete terms, that means there are seventy-two people to every toilet, and eighty to every shower. And the camp can boast the sum total of one doctor and no lawyers. Violence and despair are everyday companions for these people who have already lost everything and who find themselves crammed together in abject conditions. Only NGOs are still in a position to raise the alarm because the Moria camp has been closed to the press since the accord signed with Turkey in March 2016. On the island of Lesbos there is a total of eleven thousand migrants who are waiting for Greece to decide their fate. Some have been there for two years, and even though Turkey has helped reduce the influx of migrants, some 1,500 to 2,000 refugees entered Greece every month in 2018. Thousands of desperate people fleeing certain death and hoping that we in Europe will treat them with humanity and dignity.

Syria
Some key dates
in the conflict

For more than forty years an authoritarian regime has ruled Syria "from father to son": Bashar al-Assad succeeded his father, Hafez, as head of state in 2000. When he came to power, Syrians briefly believed their country would be liberalized, but this hope was short-lived.

2011

March: Unprecedented peaceful demonstrations in Syria with an immediate and very violent response from the regime: arrests, beatings, and live bullets fired. Assad frees dozens of jihadi prisoners from his prisons.

Summer: The summer of 2011 marks the escalation of the rebellion into armed conflict with the creation of the Free Syrian Army (FSA), initially intended to protect demonstrators from the regime's repressive activities. Jihadi groups also start emerging, independent of the FSA. The Syrian National Council (SNC) is set up and based in Turkey to coordinate the political fight against the regime. France and the United States recognize the SNC as a legitimate body in late 2011.

2012

January: The French journalist Gilles Jacquier is assassinated in Homs.

March: The regime's army takes control of the Baba Amr district, the bastion of the rebellion in Homs.

July: The FSA initiates the battle for Damascus and takes control of parts of the city's suburbs, including Ghouta, but not the capital itself. On July 20, the rebels begin the battle of Aleppo.

2013

April: Hassan Nasrallah, the leader of the Lebanese Shiite Hezbollah, decides to fight alongside the Syrian regime. Iran also decides to participate and mobilizes Iraqi and Afghan Shiite militias.

June: The regime's army sets up several headquarters across the country.

August: The regime undertakes a violent assault to reclaim Ghouta. There is outrage throughout the West because Assad uses chemical weapons in Samalka and Ain Tarma, killing 1,300 people. The possibility of military intervention is even discussed, particularly in France and the United States.

September: The idea of air strikes is abandoned in favor of a resolution from the UN Security Council. Assad is believed to have destroyed his arsenal of chemical weapons.

2014

January: FSA rebels now have to fight Islamic State jihadis from Iraq and the Levant (ISIL), who take the city of Raqqa from them before adopting the name "Islamic State" in June.

Summer: Western concern grows about the progress of Islamic State. Is it wise, as the Russians contend, to support Assad as a defense against the jihadis?

In order to stem Islamic State's progress, an international coalition of sixty states is set up at the instigation of the United States and France. The coalition bombs Islamic State positions in Iraq in August, and in northeast Syria in September.

2015

January–February: Kurds in the YPG and Peshmerga take Kobane with the support of anti–Islamic State coalition air strikes led by the United States. Control of this strategically placed city near the Turkish border helps slow the influx of jihadis from Turkey into Syria.

September: Assad's ally Russia starts a campaign of air strikes allegedly targeting terrorist groups, but Western sources claim that they mostly target the SFA and help the Assad regime, which is about to collapse, to regain territory.

The Paris public prosecutor opens an inquiry into Bashar al-Assad's crimes against humanity based on the "César" file: 50,000 photos showing at least 11,000 people who died in Syrian prisons.

2016

March: Discussions intended to bring an end to the conflict take place in Geneva.

September: A truce allows Syria to celebrate Eid al-Adha in peace, but lasts only a few weeks.

November: With US support, Arab–Kurdish forces launch a major offensive to reclaim Raqqa, Islamic State's capital in Syria, timed to coincide with an attack on Islamic State in Mosul in Iraq.

December: The Syrian regime announces that, thanks to military support from Russia and Iran, it has regained control of Aleppo, its most important victory over the rebels since the beginning of the war.

In late December 2016, a cease-fire is implemented under the aegis of Russia and Turkey but without the United States. It does not last long.

2017

April: The Syrian army attacks the Khan Shaykhun area in northwestern Syria, killing at least eighty-six people, including twenty-seven children. The use of sarin gas is reported and France calls for an emergency meeting of the UN Security Council. In the absence of an agreement, the United States unilaterally attacks a Syrian airbase, killing six people.

Over the course of the year, Islamic State progressively loses territories it has taken in Iraq and Syria, but does not withdraw altogether.

2018

February: Western Ghouta is bombed aggressively by the Syrian and Russian armies.

April: After renewed attacks generally assumed to be chemical, the regime announces that it has retaken Ghouta. These chemical attacks provoke retaliatory strikes coordinated by Paris, Washington, and London, and targeting strategic Syrian army positions.

May: The regime destroys the Palestinian refugee camp Al Yarmouk. A law is passed allowing the assets of "displaced" Syrians to be confiscated and used for reconstruction.

June: Lebanon pushes Syrian refugees on its soil (who number some 1.5 million) to return to Syria. By the end of the year, a little over 2,500 of these exiles opt to return home to a country destroyed by seven years of war.

July: Supported by his Iranian and Russian allies, Assad retakes Deraa, the symbolically significant region where the revolt started in 2011.

September–November: A demilitarized zone is instated around Idlib, under Russian and Turkish supervision. Despite this, the regime pulverizes this last rebel stronghold in the country. 50,000 fighters stand up to Assad's forces there but the strikes are a daily threat to the lives of the 3 million inhabitants (1 million of them children) crammed into the area.

The Syrian conflict has killed between 400,000 and 500,000 people, and displaced 12 million.